# CHOOSING EQUALITY
**The Case for Democratic Schooling**

# CHOOSING EQUALITY
## The Case for Democratic Schooling

Ann Bastian, Norm Fruchter, Marilyn Gittell,
Colin Greer, and Kenneth Haskins

Foreword by James P. Comer

 **Temple University Press**
Philadelphia

Temple University Press, Philadelphia 19122
Copyright © 1985, 1986 by Temple University
All rights reserved
Published 1986
Printed in the United States of America

Parts of this book were previously issued as a report
by The New World Foundation.

The paper used in this publication meets the
minimum requirements of American National
Standard for Information Sciences—Permanence of
Paper for Printed Library Materials, ANSI Z39.48-1984

Library of Congress Cataloging-in-Publication Data

Choosing equality.

   Bibliography: pp. 197–209
   Includes index.
   1. Educational equalization—United States.
2. Socially handicapped children—Education—United
States.   3. Children of minorities—Education—
United States.   I. Bastian, Ann.
LC213.2.C48   1986      370.19′34      86-5879
ISBN 0-87722-438-2 (alk. paper)
ISBN 0-87722-454-4 (pbk.)

# Preface

*Choosing Equality* is the product of a two-year project developed by The New World Foundation to advance equity issues and democratic values in the national debate over public school reform. This work was prompted by a deep concern that the prevailing trend in school improvement—often labeled the "excellence movement"—fundamentally ignores the need of those most damaged by failing schools, particularly low-income and minority children. Further, this work reflects concern that our schools are becoming increasingly devalued as public institutions essential to the quality of citizenship and community in this society. Our purpose, then, has been to examine the implications of the excellence movement and to renew the case for equality as an irreducible condition of excellence in the mission of public education.

*Choosing Equality* is a collaborative effort, involving not only the five authors but also a wide range of educators and school advocates with long-standing commitments to democratic education. We would like to thank more than forty participants in New World's Educational Visions Seminar, whose initial discussions of school practice and policy helped to frame many core issues of this report. Additional readers have provided important insights and guidance. Several national policy and advocacy networks have stimulated and encouraged our analysis, including the National Committee of Citizens in Education, the Institute for Responsive Education, the National Coalition of Advocates for Students, and the Institute for Policy Studies.

Appreciation is also due to David Ramage, past Foundation president, and to the New World Board of Directors, for their informed support throughout the drafting and publication of *Choosing Equality* and for the Foundation's continued commitment to fostering community initiatives for progressive school reform—particularly in low-income, minority, urban, and rural communities, which have historically been denied equal access, quality instruction, adequate support services, and equitable school funding.

# Contents

# Contents

Contents

# Foreword
## James P. Comer, M.D., M.P.H.

*Choosing Equality* is a welcome relief from the flurry of national reports and discussions of the "crisis in education" released in the last several years. The previous reports oversimplified the complex forces that have converged to create problems in education. Indeed, the previous reports in large part misidentify the crisis. *Choosing Equality* reopens the dialogue and offers a more realistic assessment and approach to addressing educational problems and opportunities in the late 20th and early 21st centuries.

After World War II, economic and technological developments dramatically and permanently changed the nature of American life—families, neighborhoods, and schools. Most institutions did not respond adequately or fully to the implications and realities of changed social conditions. This was particularly true of our public school system. The failure to adequately respond is the major cause of our "crisis in education" and not a loss of will or rigor as suggested in previous reports. Previous reports all but ignore the profound way in which American life has been altered and the impact of this transformation on schools; they have made narrow standards and content-oriented recommendations that cannot possibly address the educational needs of our nation now or in the future.

Prior to the mid-1940s we were a nation of townships, rural areas, and big cities, which were themselves collections of small-town neighborhoods. Work and play were usually local. As a result, parents, teachers, administrators, ministers, and policemen—most authority figures—interacted with each other or similar persons in a variety of ways. With limited mobility and information from the outside of a community, these authority figures were "the source of all truth" and they spoke with almost a "common tongue" about what was right and wrong, good and bad. The information young people received, for the most part, was censored and given to them by these "meaningful others."

Under these conditions, authority figures were powerful and influential. They were not always fair or right, but their response—and thus the environment of a child—was predictable. There was a sense of place and belonging, even if one's place was not desirable. Young people had few opportunities to act on models of behavior different from the community norm. Under these circumstances children more often accepted the authority of adults. The authoritarian approach to child rearing and managing social systems such as schools was reasonably effective.

The school was a natural part of the community. The authority of parents was passed directly to school staff. The latter were in the position to greatly influence the behavior and performance of children. Without making a conscious effort, school staff aided the growth and development of students. What most adults remember about early school in particular is not the content of the curriculum but the advice, sanctions, and support they received from a number of teachers. Success in school gave students a sense of adequacy and helped to motivate them to be responsible family members, participants in the neighborhood and community, and citizens of the society.

Despite the cohesive nature of the pre-1940s community, many, many children failed in school. Some could not meet the social and academic demands of school. Some were pushed out by social and cultural discrimination. There was no value in school for many. But leaving school in the past was not a serious problem. Most young people could go out and earn a living, take care of themselves and their families, and experience a sense of personal adequacy from being able to do so. Jobs on the farm, on the waterfront, and in the steel mills during most of the Industrial Revolution did not require a high level of academic skill.

Technology, applied in every aspect of life after 1945, speeded up our movement from an agricultural, through an industrial, and then to a service-based economy. Television gave us rapid, visual communication from across the country and around the world. Equally, if not more importantly, good roads and fast cars allowed teachers and administrators to live long distances from the children and families they served. These developments rendered neighborhood and community boundaries less fixed, important models of behavior less local.

After the mid-1940s, obtaining a desirable or "living-wage" job more often required a reasonably high floor of social and academic skills. And education became the ticket of admission to such jobs, even when they did not actually require specific academic or social skills. Economic and social support for minority education—particularly for blacks, Hispanics, and Native Americans—was very much less than that for whites.

Consequently, many more minority families were excluded from living-wage jobs and other economic opportunities because of undereducation, changing technologies, and other social policies and practices. And even when minority students were adequately educated, racial discrimination barred economic opportunity. Minority groups, as a result, have lacked the political or social power necessary to force policy-makers to be responsive to their problems and needs. In turn, a disproportionate number of poor and minority families live under stressful conditions.

Many children from families under stress did not and do not receive adequate support for growth and development along pathways necessary for school success—social, psychological, intellectual, linguistic, and so on. Most of these students are capable but underdeveloped along these critical pathways. In addition, a large number of children experience family breakup of one kind or another, or have two parents in the workforce; as a result, a growing number of middle- and upper-income children also experience inadequate development and/or inadequate support necessary for school success.

While societal conditions have changed dramatically, the training of teachers and the organization and management of schools have not changed very much at all. Most teachers and administrators do not receive even basic information about how children grow, develop, and behave, or about how school organization and management and staff behavior affect student growth, development, and behavior. What teachers and administrators receive in this area, if anything, is theoretical and abstract. They are not prepared to apply such knowledge in the school situation. When mental health and child development specialists assist them in doing so, the focus is almost always on the student as the source of the problem rather than on the organization and management of the school. Thus, school people are generally not very effective in helping underdeveloped children be successful in school. Even schools serving children who are educationally well prepared struggle with problems of disrespect for authority, vandalism, drug abuse, and the erosion of citizenship skills.

In short, it is my impression that technological and social change—combined with a lag in institutional change—precipitated our "crisis in education," or the failure of many schools to adequately address the needs of our students.

Why are conservative analysts and policy-makers pretending that teaching and learning problems are unrelated to economic, community, and family changes—and inadequate school adjustments to them? The possibilities range from a belief that low-achieving children and schools simply cannot or will not do any better to a belief that the future of the nation rests in an elitist group, that Thomas Jefferson and others who believed that education for all was the chief infrastructure of democracy were simply wrong. There appears to be an effort to institutionalize what is in some places already a two-tier public education system—first class for the affluent, second class for the poor—if not an effort to do away with most of the public education system altogether. And the push for private education appears to be in areas with large low-income and minority populations.

Whatever the reasons for not addressing issues related to change and abandoning the poor, more often minorities, it is foolhardy social policy. This nation was founded in response to the tyranny of the elite and powerful. And its best chance for survival and continued strength remains with the creation of an intelligent citizenry independent enough to respond appropriately to excesses of power. This was the founding mission of public education—not the creation of a workforce or an intellectual elite.

History, as well as today's headlines, tell us that the creation of an elite group of academic high achievers is not enough. Fairness, concern for others, and responsible person-to-person interactions are needed if a democratic society is to flourish. If such attitudes, values, and norms are not modeled in the organization and management of schools, they are less likely to be displayed in the behavior of our young as adults, even where families strive to promote them. Preparing the young to live in a democratic society and preparing them to achieve at the highest level of their individual talents are not mutually exclusive activities. Both require the creation of a school staff capable of creating a school setting and a home-school relationship that simultaneously promotes the intellectual, social, psychological, and moral development of our young.

Across the country there is promise. There are examples of schools successfully serving children from all backgrounds in racially and socio-economically separate and integrated settings. Our collaborative Yale Child Study Center–New Haven School System project—through attention to child development and relationship issues—facilitated significant improvements in academic achievement among students who were 99% black and almost all poor. Simultaneously attendance improved and behavior problems declined dramatically. The Effective Schools movement demonstrates that such projects are not idiosyncratic and that the critical success variables can be identified and institutionalized nationwide. Thus, there is clear evidence that it is possible to prepare young people for responsible citizenship and high-level academic achievement.

Previous reports ignored the profound implications and realities of the social and technological revolution we are in. It is difficult to imagine how increasing the time undermotivated children spend in a particular subject area will increase their enthusiasm for and performance in it. It is difficult to imagine how teachers who complain that students have little self-discipline or respect for authority will be better able to function in the classroom when their training emphasizes more academic content and ignores systems management, child development, and human relationships. If we do not reopen the dialogue around school improvement, we are headed for the usual cycle of events in education—the identification of a problem, a "movement" to attack the problem without an adequate analysis, a problem-solving approach that fails, disillusionment and hopelessness about public education.

Fortunately, *Choosing Equality* adds a new dimension to the school reform debate. The authors do not pretend to have "the answer." But they very effectively discredit the myths undergirding the major thrust of previous reports. They very carefully explore school practices and options for change. They speak eloquently to the need for the school to again become an integral part of the community, to serve the ends of a democratic society, to promote personal and social empowerment of the students and communities they serve.

*Choosing Equality* lays out the issues and alternatives fully, not ignoring the context of education in favor of content, methods, and standards. It calls for citizens' input to decide among the choices we have. It is citizen involvement—and not the free hand of professionals, bureaucrats, or politicians—that can make education responsive to the needs of life in our complex democracy. If the message and methods of this report are heeded, we can still create a public education system that will help prepare all of our children to function in our present and future world.

# CHOOSING EQUALITY

**The Case for Democratic Schooling**

# I.
## Making Choices

When the question is asked, "What should we do about the public schools?" it almost always means, "What should public schools do?" For the past two years, this has been the fundamental issue in the intense national debate over school reform. Beyond the focus on teacher morale or academic standards, Americans are probing the purposes of schooling, sorting out which needs schools should meet and what expectations they should fulfill.

For the general public, the debate expresses a rising fear about declining school performance and, perhaps more basically, fear about the future for youth in our society. This concern seems a natural product of recurring economic and social insecurity. The country is in the midst of profound structural shifts in technology, in job and income distribution, in family life, and in government commitments. These shifts intensify existing inequities and threaten familiar patterns of individual mobility and community cohesion. Yet the debate also expresses hope. People turn to the schools as a social tool, one of few institutions that are public and

3

local, for adapting to new demands and for protecting the coming generation.

Underlying the impulses to fear and hope is an unspoken tension between priorities for school change. We see this as a tension between two divergent goals for public education: a desire for schools to serve the competitive demands of a stratified society, and a desire for schools to play a socially integrative and democratic role, serving the right of all children to develop to their fullest potential. Some people do not see these as incompatible functions; others deny that they require different kinds of schooling. Yet choices are being made, and in the current wave of school reform, democratic values of education have given ground to competitive pressures and renewed elitism.

Since the outburst of national education reports in 1983, major initiatives for school change have fallen under the banner of the "excellence movement." While the call for excellence is universal, excellence means different things to different people. In some cases, the push for greater quality has fostered thoughtful inquiry into school problems and innovative approaches. In other cases, the excellence effort has been rhetorically benign, but regressive in its impact on school practice. And in too many cases, excellence has become a codeword for retrenchment in public education, signaling a retreat from egalitarian commitments and from public responsibility in schooling.

When we look at the concrete policies enacted in the name of excellence over the past three years, the results are not as comforting as many suppose. There are new standards for achievement, but not new resources or strategies to ensure that all children will have the appropriate means to meet these standards. There are new tests for performance, but rarely new designs to create more responsive learning environments or to combat existing patterns of rigidity, inequity, and exclusion. There is a new emphasis on accountability, but deep resistance to institutional reforms that open the schools to those they serve. In practice, the mainstream of the excellence movement ignores or dismisses the qualitative issues of equity, school culture, and the relationship of schools to communities. Such negligence is widening an alarming gap between the educational haves and havenots. It is also devaluing the school as a social institution pledged to both the personal and the civic empowerment of all citizens.

This book seeks to clarify the choices between elitist and democratic goals for public education that are being made in the 1980s. We take the position that democratic concepts of schooling should govern the direction of change and, in particular, that the massive school failure experienced in low-income communities should be of primary concern. We believe that equality in education is the inalienable right of all Americans. We believe that schools belong to citizens, not as clients but as owners of a public institution. And we believe that equality and participation in the educational process are essential conditions of educational excellence.

Yet we are also aware that our beliefs require a much firmer vision of what constitutes quality schooling and what is necessary to make quality a universal commitment than has emerged in the debate thus far. This book has, therefore, several purposes. We examine where the current thrust for school change is leading and explore alternative frameworks for understanding and addressing school failure. We look at the untapped resources available for school improvement, which range from effective instructional models, to participatory school governance, to redistributive financing. We consider what constituencies can be set in motion so that reform enlarges the democratic promise of public schooling.

We are presenting an image of the opportunities for change, not a blueprint or formula that can ensure progressive outcomes in school reform. The agenda for democratic schooling will itself be incomplete until a more active and cohesive citizens' movement develops in education. What we propose are ways of viewing the options that help break through the polarities of equity and excellence and move beyond the limits of past reform or present reaction. We try to connect what happens in the classroom to organizational and institutional contexts. We discuss the multiple levels of structural change necessary to achieve fundamental change. We explore the political processes that set priorities for education, and thus decide what we expect or tolerate in school performance.

There is the danger, of course, that such a sweeping statement of needs and issues may suggest all-or-nothing solutions. Our intent, however, is not to assert that anything short of wholesale reform cannot make a difference. Rather, we try to envision long-term goals for change that place immediate struggles for school improvement in an ongoing process, so that today's demands are consistent with an overall vision for change, so that today's advocates can build isolated victories into broader challenges. Settling for piecemeal reform does have serious limitations: the problem of winning skirmishes and losing the war. Nonetheless, systematic change can proceed in stages, if we recognize that the basic conflicts between democratic and elitist purposes in schooling are not resolved because we have gained new ground.

In surveying these multiple dimensions of school reform, we have developed the following basic arguments:

## THE MISSION OF SCHOOLING

The opening rounds of the school debate have been dominated by a neo-conservative consensus that, by design or by default, identifies excellence with an elitist concept of meritocracy. The thrust has been to reinforce competitive structures of achievement, modeled on and serving the economic marketplace. This perspective misconstrues the crisis in education, which in our view is twofold: there is a catastrophic failure to provide decent schools and adequate skills to low-income students; there is also a chronic failure to provide reasoning and citizenship skills among all students. Moreover, school failure in the bottom tiers and narrow achievement throughout the system, cited to justify meritocratic practices, are in fact the result of such practices.

In establishing a framework for progressive alternatives, it is necessary to project a concept of education in which quality and equality are mutually inclusive standards. We must answer the questions: How do we measure equality? What defines democratic education?

## THREE MYTHS OF SCHOOL PERFORMANCE

In further challenging the meritocratic framework, we examine three popular myths that underlie the neo-conservative side of the school debate. These myths serve to narrow the vision of reform and to lower the expectations placed on education, particularly its role in meeting social needs and promoting capacities for citizenship.

Myth One is that today's school failures represent a recent development, in contrast with a "golden age" of public schooling that once served well both the elite and the mass of students. But in our view, the gulf between elite and mass goals and methods of education has been a constant feature of our education system; today's failures express the tradition of an historically stratified system.

Myth Two is that the equity reforms attempted in the '60s and '70s have proven either diverting or damaging to the quest for excellence. In fact, the reforms enacted were not fully egalitarian, were actively subverted in their implementation, and have remained marginal to the education system. The reform era achieved a shift from exclusive meritocracy to inclusive meritocracy, but it did not transform the schools. Our choices are not limited to embracing either deficient reform or an elitist backlash; we can also choose to pursue more fundamental change.

Myth Three is that national economic growth and individual mobility are contingent on establishing more rigorous standards of education competition. Yet current economic trends contradict the notion that education will fuel economic recovery and broadly distribute economic rewards. The employment functions of schooling do not constitute a sufficient mechanism or rationale for structuring educational goals.

## SCHOOL PRACTICE: INGREDIENTS OF EFFECTIVE INSTRUCTION

If we seek to address the crisis of inequality that has meant school failure for the poor, and seek to improve the citizenship capacities of all students, we must refocus the debate over classroom reforms. Prevailing prescriptions for school improvement tend to swing between hard and soft ap-

8

proaches—poles expressed by calls to restore authority and toughen standards or, conversely, by the reflex to defend the neglect and lowered expectations that too often pass for "appropriate" education. These approaches ignore what is deeply flawed in the traditional structures of the learning environment: the neglect of critical inquiry, the isolation of teachers and segregation of students, inappropriate uses of time and testing, rigidity in response to diverse needs, the fragmentation and denial of supportive services.

Technical approaches, stressing reward-or-punish models of accountability for both teachers and students, offer more of the same. Yet there are alternative models that tell us a great deal about the ingredients of effective instruction. Common to each is the construction of flexible, collaborative, and human-scale school environments and a clear commitment to equality of need. These models indicate that a systematic restructuring of school organization is necessary, in mainstream education as much as in programs to meet special needs, in suburban as well as in ghetto schools.

## SCHOOL CONSTITUENCIES: DIRECTIONS FOR CHANGE

To secure progressive changes in instruction, it is essential to go beyond the classroom focus and to challenge the arrangements of institutional power that subvert responsive education. School systems are typically constructed to deny parents, teachers, and communities a positive role in guiding school practice. These frontline constituencies are vital both as resources for school improvement and as activists for democratic priorities in the reform process. But it is often the case, particularly in the most deprived school systems, that parents are regularly excluded from participating in school affairs and even blamed for student failure. Teachers are frequently viewed as caretakers and technicians, denied control over their working conditions and their professional development by the lack of supportive resources, by bureaucratic professionalism, by autocratic management. And schools, especially the worst schools, remain isolated from and often antagonistic toward the communities they serve.

The educational value of schools that empower their constituents and function as community institutions can be clearly demonstrated. Pursuing this goal on a broad scale, however, quickly raises the problem of making such reforms tangible, not token. We look at four topical issues that are proving important in defining our concept of the school as an open institution: voucher or optional enrollment systems, the Effective Schools movement, community-based literacy campaigns, and youth service programs.

## GOVERNANCE AND FUNDING:
## TOWARD PROGRESSIVE FEDERALISM

Progressive reforms in the structures of education will not go far without addressing the fundamental governance and funding mechanisms that set the bottom lines for school priorities. In the face of conservative attempts to reduce government commitments, and with policy increasingly in the hands of bureaucrats and professionals, it is important to rethink our goals for federal, state, and local authority in education. We propose a concept of progressive federalism, altering the role of each level of government to promote the redistribution of resources and power in school institutions.

We advocate that the local school become the center of decision-making, involving parents and communities, as well as frontline educators, in control over budget and policy. Recognizing state government as the pivotal arena for school change, we argue for a more strategic effort to reform funding formulas and standards; we project an activist state role in redressing the pervasive disparities in school revenues and in promoting local governance. We look to a federal role that enlarges both funding and mandates for educational equality. In formulating these potentials for progressive federalism, we affirm our belief that public education is not wholly bound by the powerful influences of social and economic stratification; the public sector can be shaped to serve democratic purposes, even as it contends with structural inequalities in society at large.

## BUILDING A NEW AGENDA

Taken as a whole, this book rejects the notion of a one best reform or a one best school system. It is an effort to clarify the choices before us and the steps that promote or deter democratic purposes in education. Reviewing the major issues of the current debate, we look not only to specific proposals but to the context in which they are offered: Are they seen as panaceas or as leverage points for restructuring? Do they substitute for fundamental changes or move toward them? Do they pre-empt the empowerment of school constituents or enlarge their capacities to shape policy in practice?

The school debate of the 1980s is far from over. While we question many of the initiatives launched in the name of excellence, the current excellence movement has at least focused public attention on the conditions of schooling. As a result, new voices have entered the debate, both through the political process and from within our troubled schools. A broader vision of alternatives is being forged, in defense of past gains and in support of new models. This book seeks to further enlarge our sense of opportunity and possibility by looking beyond the alarm over the school crisis, by moving toward a democratic conception of the public school mission, and by posing the priorities for change that democratic education demands.

# 2.

## The Mission of Schooling

The public concern touched off by the school debate of the past three years may not be well focused, but it is well founded. Our public schools are not adequately endowing students with the knowledge and reasoning skills they need and, for many, school performance has been disastrous. But the roots of this crisis are not self-evident. Indeed, the character and location of the crisis are crucial issues of the debate, since whoever shapes the definition of the problem will also shape the solutions pursued.

### THE RIGHT'S AGENDA

The current ferment in public education arises within a national climate of resurgent conservatism. Education, as a basic feature of the American social contract and the largest public entitlement program, also becomes an arena for intense ideological and political contention. Both the Old and the New Right have taken the initiative in redirecting the education debate with the same objectives that guide their economic and social welfare policies: to reduce government responsibility for social needs, to reinforce competitive structures of mobility, to lower expectations for security, and to popularize Social Darwinist thinking.

The Right has identified school failures with what it perceives as the twin evils of excessive egalitarianism and oppressive public sector intervention. The first premise is stated succinctly in a report from the Heritage Foundation, a key advisory group to the Reagan administration, which declares: "For the past twenty years, federal mandates have favored 'disadvantaged' pupils at the expense of those who have the highest potential to contribute to society."[1] The goal of rolling back the public sector is made equally clear by the president's Marshner Commission, which in its 1982 report on school finance proposed deep cuts in federal aid to equity programs and expanding the role of private education.[2] This perspective has been consistently reinforced by the Reagan's Department of Education, under its present secretary, William Bennett. Bennett and his DOE colleagues have been highly visible in attacking special education for the handicapped, bilingual education, student loan programs, and the Supreme Court's *Felton* decision, which restricted the rising flow of federal categorical aid to private schools.

The administration's agenda is backed by a political coalition of ultra-conservatives, religious fundamentalists, and entrepreneurs, who are intent on displacing public education with a private marketplace for schooling. Ideologically, such conservatives oppose the notion that there is a public interest in education that cannot be effectively advanced or protected through competitive self-interest and profit motives. Moreover, such conservatives see public school institutions as imposing intolerable restraints on individual

14

will by maintaining the separation of church and state, by mandating standards of non-discrimination, and by embodying values of secular pluralism. To them, public education is not an expression of the social contract, but, in their own words, a "monopoly" to be broken apart.

The ideological Right has taken up its war against public education on many fronts, pressing for the reinstatement of school prayer and mounting censorship campaigns against the teaching of evolution and other humanist features of modern curricula. But its most serious and concerted offensive has been to push tuition tax credits and voucher systems that open the gates for public aid to private education. The Right's failure to win broad support for tuition tax credits in the past five years should not be cause for complacency. Recognizing widespread public mistrust of openly elitist privatization schemes, rightwingers have wrapped their plans in new packages.

The new approach to privatization is exemplified by the Reagan administration's Equity and Choice Act (TEACH), introduced in 1985 to reverse the *Felton* decision legislatively. The bill would allow federal Chapter 1 funds, now financing public compensatory education programs for low-income children, to be converted into lump-sum vouchers that eligible families can apply to private school tuition. If enacted, the bill would gut Chapter 1, which is among the most successful of federal equity programs, which injects desperately needed monies into distressed public school systems, and which has been a target for Reagan cutbacks since 1980. Under TEACH, public school Chapter 1 programs would be thrown into fiscal disarray. At the same time, private schools receiving voucher subsidies would be exempt from the mandates of the 1964 Civil Rights Act and would be subject to the most perfunctory public oversight.

The rhetoric behind TEACH claims that it will serve social justice in three ways: by harnessing market incentives to improve Chapter 1 performance, by honoring parents' rights to determine the type of school their children attend, and by granting "disadvantaged families some of the educational choices already available to more affluent families."[3] It is more than ironic that the erosion of public compensatory programs so efficiently carried out by the Reagan administration has now become the virtuous excuse for dismantling such programs—and stripping bare the only institutions that poor people can realistically afford or hold accountable.

While it is unlikely that TEACH or some equivalent will make much headway in Congress, a new series of voucher plans lie beyond it. Using the same camouflage of equity and parental rights, a self-proclaimed choice movement is promoting tuition voucher systems at the state level, across party lines. The choice movement aims to include private schools, as in Colorado's Second Chance Program. If that fight is premature, the choice movement proceeds with public school voucher plans, with preference for statewide vouchers, as recently adopted in Minnesota. In either version, the concept of a competitive marketplace in education has triumphed over the idea that every local school system should be decent, accessible, capable of offering options, and committed to meeting diverse needs. Moreover, the concept of the parent as the isolated consumer of a retail product has triumphed over the principle that parents and citizens are joint owners of community-based institutions. As we discuss more fully in Chapter 5, choice in itself means little if the public cannot control what alternatives are available.

The dangers posed by the privatization strategies of the

Right deserve greater scrutiny and alarm than they have received in the public debate thus far. For even if tuition credits and voucher plans are defeated for the moment, the federal divestiture of resources in public education and the retreat from equity standards set up a dangerously self-fulfilling prophecy. If these trends intensify, public schooling will undereducate growing numbers of children and will increasingly lose public confidence. In this case, Social Darwinist solutions—salvaging special schools for the "best and the brightest," segregating disadvantaged segments of the student population, subsidizing private school alternatives, establishing market mechanisms of service delivery—will appear more justified and feasible, especially when clothed in the rhetoric of personal opportunity and choice.

Nor should we underestimate the influence of the Right on present educational content. The fact that a major education publisher, Doubleday and Sons, could issue a junior high school biology textbook without one reference to the word "evolution"—and that the State of California had to reject every other biology text submitted for adoption because none dealt adequately with the topic—should signal that the Right has at least achieved a climate of intimidation.

Finally, the Right's frontal assault on the values and institutions of public education is disturbing in the ways it has diverted the mainstream of educational policy. Public education advocates have spent extraordinary energy and resources in rearguard actions to contain the Right's agenda and minimize the damage. More seriously, the Right has given added credibility and political presence to more measured voices that, while defending the public nature of our education system, nonetheless propose to strengthen its elitist features. In this sense, the frontal attack has opened the way for backdoor attacks that, in our view, pose the most enduring, fundamental challenge to the democratic mission of American public schooling.

## The Neo-Conservative Agenda

Very few education experts or policy advisors outside the present Reagan administration endorse the rightwing agenda for privatization, cutbacks, and censorship. All of the major national task forces that have issued reports since 1983—including the Bell Commission, the Business–Higher Education Forum, the Twentieth Century Fund, and the Council on Economic Development—call for sustained federal funding and affirm the commitment to a free, universal public education system.

Yet the most influential of these reports[4] have forged a consensus that promotes a basic conservative premise: school improvement hinges on a more standardized, more regimented, more competitive approach. The consensus defines mediocrity as the key problem in American schooling and identifies low standards of achievement as its main cause. This viewpoint provides the foundation for what has become the central thrust of today's excellence movement and a neo-conservative vision of school change.

Of course, not all the reports on current school problems fall within the neo-conservative camp. A number of in-depth, qualitative studies—such as the work of John Goodlad and Theodore Sizer[5]—present a very different picture of what is wrong in school practice and repudiate "get-tough" prescriptions for excellence. The National Coalition of Advocates for Students' report, based on nationwide public hearings, stresses the inequities that structure school failure.[6] The report of the Committee for Economic Development, a council of business leaders, stresses the need for greater flexibility in teaching and for participatory school management.[7] Yet these voices have not been widely heeded beyond academic and teaching circles. The public debate and the legislative policy agenda have thus far been dominated by neo-conservative positions, with these common arguments:

1. The crisis in education is most seriously identified by declining achievement levels of college-bound students and by a shortage of the highly skilled personnel needed to maintain America's competitive economic and technological advantage in world markets.

2. This decline in achievement and basic skills is attributed to schools' having recently become permissive, eclectic, and distracted by inappropriate social demands. The problem is characterized by Diane Ravitch, a member of the Twentieth Century Fund Task Force, as a pervasive "loss of authority," stemming from "confused ideas, irresolute standards," and cultural relativism.[8]

3. Reform efforts should concentrate on a return to academic basics and more rigorous demands on student and teacher performance. The program calls for standardizing pedagogy and curriculum, mandating more time on core curriculum, restricting non-academic "frills," increasing the use of standardized and competitive testing to pre-sort and track students, lengthening the school day and year, legislating more stringent promotion and graduation requirements. Proposals for improving teaching quality center on merit pay, master teacher programs, and test-based competency measures. A number of proposals also promote corporate models of school management and an emphasis on economic development goals.

This book will examine each of these issues and how well

they serve effective education. But more important than any single prescription is that the overall neo-conservative thrust has shifted public concern away from the institutional basis of school failure. The traditional structures of the classroom and school management are not questioned. The problems of excessive hierarchy and bureaucracy, of sorting children according to their labor market destinies, of impersonal and passive learning environments are not raised as determinant conditions of teacher and student performance. Indeed, the traditional instructional and institutional arrangements of education are addressed only by the assumption that they should be more strenuously reconstructed.

More critically, public concern has also been shifted away from social and political issues that are central to equality in education. The volumes that have announced a crisis in our schools do not talk much about the gross disparities in school funding, the discriminatory impacts of what and how we teach, the isolation of schools from their communities, and, above all, the denial of access to effective schooling that persists for millions of American schoolchildren.

## Elitism versus Equity

Whether the "basics" are defined from a fundamentalist or humanist or vocational perspective, the back-to-basics movement does not make equality a condition of quality. For some, the intent is explicit. Many neo-conservatives view the egalitarian demands of social movements in the '6os and '7os as directly responsible for today's school crisis, for what they perceive as a dilution of standards and purpose. It is not far from the Heritage Foundation position to the well-publicized pronouncement of the Twentieth Century Fund Task Force that "[government] emphasis on promoting equality of opportunity has meant a slighting of its commitment to educational quality."[9]

Other national reports are careful to affirm the principle that reform must bring excellence to all, but they have failed to offer any substantive proposals for correcting unequal educational and social conditions. Harold Howe notes that none of the recent commission reports mentions the landmark *Brown v. Board of Education* decision, and comments, "Clearly there is little remaining commitment to the idea that separate and unequal schools are unacceptable and not enough commitment to equal opportunity to elicit clear and specific recommendations on how these crucial goals are to be pursued."[10] Perhaps it is assumed that these battles are over, that the channels for achieving equality are already open, that the mechanisms for compensating disadvantage are already in place. If so, it is a premise that defies the reality of rising economic, social, and educational deprivation in our society. In schooling, as elsewhere, the gap between the haves and have-nots is growing.

What this initiative in education amounts to is an attempt to reconstruct the elitist form of meritocracy that has long prevailed in our education system. Along the way, a number of classic conventions about the school mission have been revived and synthesized. The social value of public education is equated with and promoted through its market value. Schools are seen to serve society primarily by supplying human capital, by underwriting the promise of individual success in competitive labor markets and national success in competitive global markets.

At the same time, the egalitarian goals of education are reduced to their narrowest definition. Uniformity and standardization are considered sufficient conditions of equality. Since each child presumably encounters the same basic program, each presumably has an equal opportunity for success. Today's elite theorists are thus drawn to the "common curriculum" model established in the 19th century. From this view follow other assumptions. Enrollment is considered the equivalent of access. Selective advancement is considered the key to motivation, supplemented with strong doses of authority as an equivalent for high expectations. Each student and teacher is given a "chance" to progress on the basis of merit, according to codified measures of achievement.

Aspiration and merit are assumed to bridge the gap between unequal resources and high achievement. Where students do not display merit, where they do not meet the standards applied evenly to all, it may be concluded that failure is a matter of individual choice or deficiency. What we have arrived at is another incentive-and-punishment system, guided by the "invisible hand" of competition.

By focusing on an economic bottom line, by narrowing their concern to accountability and basics, by ignoring the realities of inequity, the prevailing school critics do warn us of a grave social risk. But the risk they signal is that new standards of merit will become in practice new mechanisms of stratification and, ultimately, another means for pushing unwanted students out of the system. Massive school failure for the other half is not the core crisis that the meritocrats choose to address in their vision for change.

## WHERE IS THE CRISIS IN PUBLIC EDUCATION?

The picture presented by neo-conservatives, and widely supported by the national commission reports, tells us that American education has suffered wholesale deterioration, threatening the highest levels of student achievement and, in the long run, our ability to compete internationally. Though the reports assume that the evidence for a severe decline is conclusive, the data they present to demonstrate such slippage are actually quite ambiguous.

Most of the commissions, for example, cite the persistent fall of SAT scores throughout the '70s, but fail to mention that SAT scores have stabilized and actually started to rise in the past few years. Moreover, recent research argues that the SAT decline is far more closely related to the sizeable expansion of the student population taking the tests—and especially the increase in working class, poor, and minority students seeking college entrance—than to any significant erosion of student ability.[11] Dispassionate analysis of SAT data might well conclude that our schools are improving the academic ability of a much broader and more diverse group of high school test-takers.

The most sensational news from the reports has been the low achievement ratings of American children compared with their counterparts in Japan and Western Europe. Yet this too bears closer scrutiny, in terms of what the tests measure and who is tested. European countries have more selective and exclusive secondary education systems, practice early occupational tracking, and have much less extensive higher education systems. The reports took no note that their comparisons involved very different school populations, which experience different learning sequences and different outcomes. Nor did the reports note comparable deficiencies in foreign systems, or account for the different social goals vested in public education.

In any case, the argument becomes spurious with regard to competitive economic advantage. The same test results used to indict American education actually show that the top 9% of American students did just as well as their counterparts in Europe and Japan.[12] These high achievers are typically upper middle class, college-bound students who supply the high-skill occupations in professional, technical, and managerial fields. Labor supply and demand may work somewhat unevenly, but there are no critical skill shortages looming in the professions that are crucial to economic development. Ironically, the most severe professional shortage in the next five years is likely to be teachers—which accurately reflects the profession's low economic standing. Moreover, affluent school systems will be able to cream the existing teacher supply to serve the upper strata of public education. Overall, the United States has more than a sufficient pool of basic and professional skills to sustain a technologically sophisticated economy. The more pressing issue is whether the economy will generate sufficient job demand to sustain its future workforce.

## A Crisis of Citizenship

This is not to say that all is well with American school achievement, currently or in the past. The issue is not only whether test scores are rising or falling, or some of both, but whether students are learning how to think, how to observe, how to analyze causes and evaluate effects, how to extract knowledge from information. This is not a concern dictated only by labor market functions, but also by the social demands of democratic citizenship. By this standard, it appears that even privileged schools, with high-ranking test scores and highly employable graduates, are not performing satisfactorily. One part, then, of the public school crisis is our inattention to social education and critical thinking skills, a failing that appears to affect all segments of the system.

The interpretive studies of American high schools recently conducted by John Goodlad, Theodore Sizer, and Ernest Boyer underscore this conclusion.[13] Their work indicates that even in relatively advantaged systems, students are not acquiring the conceptual and problem-solving skills that are the basis for critical thinking and self-motivation. Goodlad and Sizer find school problems that stem not from the loss of discipline or dilution of standards, but from school environments that are restrictive, impersonal, organizationally rigid, and understaffed. They find that teachers are isolated, overworked, stripped of the autonomy and interaction they need to be innovative and engaged. They find that traditional classroom management discourages student initiative, while routinized curriculum engenders passivity and distance.

These critiques support the case for "opening up, rather than clamping down."[14] In signaling the failure to cultivate independent inquiry and analytic skills, they point to a dimension of school deficiency that will only be reinforced by the meritocratic emphasis on standardization, testing, and back-to-basics. This failure in public education is not necessarily dysfunctional in economic terms. Cynics could argue that dull minds are more compatible with the production and consumption roles that await most of today's children. However, the incapacity for critical thinking is likely to ensure this dreary outcome of limited futures and narrow function for the mass of students. Our failure to create an informed and thoughtful citizenry will also have continuing impact on our quality of life as a culture and as a society that aspires toward democratic pluralism. It is difficult to judge whether schools have declined in areas of cognitive and affective learning, but it is clear that task-oriented conceptions of rigor will discourage their improvement.

## A Crisis of Inequality

There is, however, a far more fundamental crisis in our schools. It is located where it has always been, in the bottom layers of a multi-tiered system, in our failure to provide even minimal levels of quality to the school population that is working class and poor. This crisis can be measured by some stark statistics: 50–80% of all inner-city students drop out of high school, one million teenagers cannot read above third-grade level, 13% of all seventeen-year-olds are functionally illiterate, 28% of all students do not get high school diplomas, 50% of college entrants drop out in their first year, one-third of all adults are functionally or marginally illiterate.[15]

In New York City today, two-thirds of all elementary school students entering public high school test below grade level. An independent study of drop-outs, conducted by ASPIRA of New York for the four years ending in June 1983, found that 68% of all public high school students fail to graduate, with a rate of 80% for Hispanic students, 72% for blacks, and 50% for whites. Other figures show that 80% of teenage mothers drop out, and 90% of all special education students do not graduate.[16]

In Chicago, a recent survey of forty-four non-selective, four-year high schools, each with over 50% black and Hispanic enrollment, showed that only 39% of entering freshmen were in school by their senior year. Of that 39% reaching the twelfth grade, 41% were below minimum proficiency (ninth-grade reading level), 41% were at or above ninth-grade proficiency but were below the national median for seniors, and only 18% were finishing high school at or above the national median. The results, by no means atypical for urban school systems, indicate that only 7% of students entering these high schools graduated with achievement levels equal to 50% of their peers nationwide.[17]

School failure for lower-income students, particularly minority students, has reached epidemic proportions. The crisis in public education has not developed because we have short-changed those at the top, but because we have grossly disserved those on the bottom. The taproot of this failure is chronic inequality in the school resources allocated to poor and declining communities, in the ways that learning is stratified and structured, in the ways schools treat diverse needs and potentials. The meritocratic framework does not acknowledge the location or nature of this crisis. Its narrow and selective prescriptions erect new barriers to achievement on top of those that have already produced catastrophic results. As we will argue more fully in the next chapter, to reinforce meritocratic practices is to promote the causes, not the correctives, of second-class schooling.

The demand for equality in education is thus not a diversion from or an afterthought to the call for excellence. The demand for equality is a call to address the real crisis in our public schools, the institutional incapacity to respond fairly or adequately to at least one-third of the nation's schoolchildren. For equality is an objective condition of effective schooling, just as inequality is a determining condition of the present crisis. But since there is more than one way to define equality, the principle itself becomes a battleground in the current school reform debate.

## EQUALITY AS A PRINCIPLE
## OF DEMOCRATIC SCHOOLING

Our discussion of the meritocratic framework raises fundamental issues about the concepts of equality that underlie our expectations for schooling. There is a prevailing notion that equality means sameness. In its most negative implications, this concept suggests that the pursuit of equality necessitates a leveling down—that equal education will produce, actually has produced, pervasive mediocrity.

Another implication is that the commitment to equality can be satisfied by offering each child the same structures of opportunity that, formally at least, make opportunity universally accessible. Those who see equality in uniformity do not fully acknowledge that, in America, children of different social classes and races are rarely provided with the same quality of schools, the same levels of expenditure per pupil, the same level of expectations for achievement. They disregard the fact that children enter the schools with very unequal societal conditions influencing their performance. They ignore the fact that programs which work well for all children are not provided to all children, and that services which counteract disadvantage are least available to the disadvantaged. The ideal of the "same chance" means only that all children are granted formal access to school enrollment. And the same chance, regardless of unfair resources for utilizing that chance, is how "equal opportunity" and "equity" are generally defined today.

This narrow standard of equality is so readily adopted because a deeper trade-off is at work. In America, schools are paradoxically expected to support the economic market system, with its inherently competitive opportunities and unequal outcomes, and to promote social democracy, with universal empowerment. The goals of the marketplace and of democracy have never been very compatible—they can become outright antagonistic in time of economic stress. These contradictory missions of schooling create enduring polarities in our education system between selective and collective achievement, between individual and community advancement, between hierarchic and participatory governance, and, in today's formulation, between excellence and equity.

The narrow definition of equal chances ostensibly resolves the tension between the dual missions of schooling by endorsing universal access, while enforcing competitive mechanisms for achievement and advancement. The fact that these mechanisms consistently reward the advantaged and hold back the disadvantaged is obscured by viewing the process as the free competition of individuals. When a child rises through the system, our notion of democratic mobility is affirmed. When a child fails—or simply fails to do well—this lack of achievement can be attributed to personal, or perhaps cultural, deficiencies; stratification seems justified and a given rate of failure seems acceptable. Schools are not expected to be as ruthlessly exclusive as the economic marketplace, but are also not expected to serve children according to their needs. The compromise in our concept of equality is that inclusion—entering the race—constitutes sufficient opportunity. The persistence of gross differentials in achievement is then made a question of personal merit.

But what works as a rationale for meritocracy—for formally inclusive elitism—masks how limited that inclusion is in practice and how disastrous the cumulative results are among youth. After several years of meritocratic school reform, reports from the grassroots—from groups like the Chapter I Parent Coalition, the National Coalition of Advocates for Students, the National Committee for Citizens in Education, the Commission of State Planning Agencies, and many others—document regressive trends in nearly every area of school service directed to the disadvantaged. More rigid standards, more specialized tasks, more segregated placements, more selective advancement are placing more children at risk.

## Equality of Results

To deal with these consequences, we need to set different standards, which measure our commitment to equality by the results—by where children come out instead of where they start. In education, equality of results means that different needs count equally in determining the expectations, resources, and services devoted to helping each child learn. Schools should be endowed with the necessary means to enable all students to be literate, employable, socially informed, and politically enfranchised, capable of participating in community life and of developing their own particular talents and interests. And while there is no simple, quantitative test for each of these goals, particularly the goals of citizenship, it is not difficult to see how far we are from achieving any of them.

From a fully democratic perspective, therefore, we interpret the concepts of equal opportunity and equity quite differently. They should not only mean the right to be included in the system, but the right to stay in the system and be provided the appropriate conditions for learning. If equality of result is the goal, equal opportunity requires a continuum of means as well as chances, which are extended, not exhausted, by obstacles to learning.

To recast the debate over school change, this book explicitly measures school performance by the equality of results.

We reject the assumption that children fail because of their own deficits; instead, we expect schools to seek merit in every child and to teach children according to their needs. We reject the premise that trade-offs between excellence and equity are inevitable; instead, we see excellence and equity as irreducible conditions of each other. We reject that the alternative to quality for the favored few is egalitarian mediocrity or worse; instead, we identify the ways in which quality can be made available to all. We recognize real conflicts between economic and social bottom lines, and go beyond the marketplace to define the national interest in schooling.

Finally, we respond to the new elitists and the new fatalists by demonstrating that democratic education is a product of social choices. After decades of trial and advance in public schooling, we now know many of the elements of effective education, in both advantaged and disadvantaged circumstances. It is a question of priorities whether this understanding is applied as a privilege or a universal right.

# 3.

## Three Myths of School Performance

The democratic purpose of American public education may be far from realized, but it is at least an ideal that most Americans value. Nearly every strategy for school change therefore claims to have universal application and benefit. In the current wave of reform, that claim to universality rests on the promise of reversing economic decline by restoring educational productivity. The idea has great appeal for a wide range of people, both middle and working class, who see a dramatic shrinkage of jobs, incomes, and chances for upward mobility and who feel increasingly powerless to control their occupational destiny or improve the quality of life for their children.

However, attaching this insecurity to a program for more punitive, restrictive, competitive schooling requires several leaps of logic. Education's neo-conservatives have constructed their argument by asserting that economic performance is closely linked to school performance. They have asserted that there is a pervasive drop in academic achievement of recent origins, which impairs our national standing in a technologically driven world economy. They have presumed that a basic cause of this decline is permissive schooling and a dilution of quality, engendered by the misguided egalitarian reforms of the '60s and '70s. And they have characterized these reforms as undermining an education system that previously provided Americans with a rigorous foundation of skills and knowledge and, in doing so, advanced the nation to the forefront of economic productivity and well-being. In their view, the United States was on top because our schools worked well; now we are falling behind because we devalued education with corrosive or utopian social demands.

It is a tidy package, powerful in its simplicity, straightforward in its formula for change, and echoed in nearly every arena of national politics. Social conditions amplify the message: rightfully or not, competition is the order of the day and no one can afford to stand aside, or set their children apart, from the scramble for dwindling opportunities. So the assumptions of the new elitists find multiple points of resonance and their construction of school history becomes the standard text.

Challenging the elitist framework requires an alternative explanation of how the crisis in education emerged: What model for success does traditional schooling really offer? What was the impact of equity reforms in the '60s and '70s? What connection does schooling have to our economic status? Defining a democratic mission for schooling requires that we set our history straight, exposing what have become the great myths of school performance.

## I. THE MYTH OF A GOLDEN AGE

Today's school problems are continuously presented by way of contrast with the notion that our schools used to work well. We hear about the *loss* of authority, the *rise* of mediocrity, the *watering down* of curricula, the *lowering* of standards, the *decline* of achievement. The exact location of past school success seems to vary according to the particular remedy proposed. But whatever the specific reference, a common image emerges.

The image of the "golden age" suggests that there were once public schools that provided the masses of American children with solid basic skills and sound work and study habits. The image suggests that these schools were the basis for a disciplined, motivated, and highly productive workforce, which made possible an unprecedented degree of economic development and mobility. Universal public education is especially credited with the advance of immigrant groups. Further, it is suggested that our schools have been a key to social integration, effectively drawing diverse peoples into the mainstream of American civic culture, forming the bedrock of democratic pluralism. Had such a school system ever existed, with such astonishing social returns, the condition of schooling today would indeed represent a catastrophic loss—and might well have captured national attention sooner than 1983.

But today's schools do not function in ways radically different from their predecessors, although important changes have occurred in school populations, in the duration of schooling, and in the social and economic context within which schools operate. It is, in fact, the failure of schools to adapt to these external changes by redefining their mission that is part of the problem. While we cannot recount the

34

complex evolution of schooling here, we can present a very different reading of the character of the "golden age" and the legacy it has left.

The traditional school system prior to World War II was a rigidly two-tiered system, with separate and unequal schools. This system had two distinct missions: to provide a rising professional middle class with academic proficiency and preparation for mobility, and to provide the poor and working class with custody and preparation for the low-wage industrial labor market. The public schools of the privileged were decent and well-endowed institutions—they were the models that today's myths universalize to prove past school success. The schools of the masses, however, were little more than holding pens, promoting high failure rates among the children of the lower strata. Many children remained outside the system, shut out by child labor, by the lack of classroom space, by language and cultural barriers, by schools that were distant or seasonal.

Mass education in its first half-century does not make today's failures look exceptional. Drop-out figures cited in urban school surveys conducted in the early 1900s are nearly identical to the figures cited in the 1979–83 Chicago survey, although the incidence of failure was more likely to be at the elementary school level; some estimates project that in the 1930s two-thirds of American students did not finish high school.[1] Descriptions of traditional mass schooling present the familiar features of educational inequality: intense overcrowding, overworked and underpaid staff, grim and decaying facilities, insufficient and arcane textbooks, ethnic and racial hostility, vast disparities in funding. The socialization that occurred was not a lesson in democratic values, but a convincing exposure to the hard realities of competition and social stigma. Repeatedly, the concept of meritocracy served to bridge the gap between elitist practice and democratic promise, by justifying the application of double standards, by presuming that the disadvantaged were deficient rather than underserved.

There were, of course, intense battles waged by the disenfranchised to gain more widespread inclusion in the promise of education. There was also concern among civic reformers that the abysmal conditions in mass schooling would contribute to social division and unrest. But in opening up the schools between 1900 and 1940, the basic two-tier structure was never challenged. Schools remained instruments of socio-economic competition, even as the number of competitors expanded. The most significant change of the period was the introduction of free public high schools, a reform largely stimulated by the middle class need to acquire secondary education and to defray its growing costs through the public treasury. High schools, and certainly academic high school programs, were not widely accessible to working class and poor students. Elementary school preparation was poor and high school entrance was selective. In effect, the high school diploma upped the educational ante, with the result that elementary education became more truly universal and, at the same time, more devalued.

## Expanding the Hierarchy

This pattern of school reform has held for eighty years: the pressure for inclusion has been accommodated by gradually increasing access to established levels of schooling, while elite status has been preserved by adding new layers that only the middle classes could widely attain. In the process, the lower levels are universalized and devalued, both in terms of the range of instruction and in terms of the labor market value of educational attainment. In addition, the extension of public schooling has always been accompanied by rigorous sorting mechanisms within each level. Sharp differentials were maintained in the quality of individual schools and in the vocational tracks to which children were assigned on the basis of their class, ethnicity, race, sex, physical and cultural attributes. What the real history of the "golden age" tells us is not surprising: public education has never transcended social or economic stratification; it has merely reproduced it. There were democratic gains, but they extended only the narrowest forms of equal opportunity and did not outpace or overcome the elitist dynamic of school institutions.

What, then, of the immigrant children who rose from rags to at least Middle American comfort? The myth celebrates the rise of the immigrants as the triumph of public education. But a closer look at this history also tells a different story. In the industrial age, until mid-century, only a select group of immigrant children reached the professional or corporate elite and usually *after* their parents had acquired middle class status within the ethnic community, if not beyond it. In the more exceptional cases, when ethnic children made it up the educational ladder without economic security, they were likely to have come from backgrounds where literacy was well-established. As happens today, schools confirmed pre-existing advantages, but did not generally succeed where those advantages were absent. Among the ethnic working class, mobility has been more a factor of jobs and income, of unionization or political patronage, than a reflection of the value of their schooling.[2]

The inequities and devaluation of mass education were not so apparent, however, during periods of economic growth and, particularly, during the 1945–65 boom that absorbed the schoolchildren of the '30s. Economic expansion extended the layers of schooling and pushed the general base of attainment and duration of schooling upward. Job growth helped to mask and mitigate school failure by assimilating drop-outs and displaced workers into blue-collar and service employment, which afforded training and promotional opportunities on the job. With the significant exception of marginal workers, minorities, and women, who remained firmly fixed on the bottom, prosperity did raise absolute living standards and income mobility, with only minimal relation to the educational credentials of the workforce.

The historic irony is that as minorities and the poor began to fight successfully for access to secondary and advanced education in the late '60s, prolonged economic expansion gave way to prolonged stagnation. But the myth of education as a springboard for economic advance and a catalyst for economic growth was not thereby dispelled. Instead, it is now assumed that what is wrong with the schools is what is new about them—the influx of disadvantaged minorities and their demands for egalitarian reform. What has been the historic failure of mass education is most readily attributed to its latest victims.

## 2. THE MYTH OF EGALITARIAN REFORM

We have argued that the traditional school system, as it entered the reform era of the 1960s, had proven far more effective in imposing its two-tier model on an enlarged system of public education than it was in generalizing excellence. The 1960s school reform movement constituted a direct challenge to that legacy, not only a battle for access to all layers of public education but also a battle to make equality of result the standard for school performance.

What was and was not achieved by this thrust toward democratic reform in the '60s and '70s is at the heart of the school debate in the 1980s. The new elite theorists of education have centered much of their argument on discrediting the egalitarian impulses of the last two decades. They have propagated the notion that '60s reforms have undermined the model of traditional school success, are either responsible for the present crisis or make no real contribution toward solving it. Curiously, this perspective generates two different interpretations of the impact of the '60s school change movement. In one version, equity demands were translated into powerful reforms, determining the context in which schooling is presently conducted. The result, in this view, has been the dilution of quality and the reduction of competency standards. In another version, equity demands produced reforms that had negligible impact on eradicating educational disadvantage. The conclusion is that equity reforms are not worth pursuing and, further, that the problems of unequal education are not within the province of schools to remedy.

Neither conclusion is correct. Nonetheless, many progressives feel trapped in the uncomfortable bind of defending previous reforms as hard-won responses to egalitarian demands, when those reforms were, for the most part, limited compromises. Moreover, even these minimal reforms have been continuously eroded in the past ten years by inadequate implementation or outright subversion. Advocates for more, not less, democratic education have been caught in a complicated middle between the failures of the old liberalism and the dangers of the new conservatism.

To move outside these two poles, we need to recognize the value of the gains that were made and the limitations of the compromises that were accepted. The reforms of the '60s and early '70s were positive in that they moved us a few steps beyond the bleak "golden age" of exclusive meritocracy, a few steps toward a more democratic mission for schooling. These reforms brought new populations into the system, enlarged expectations for equality, introduced federal relief funds, and established several models for more effective education. These same reforms proved deficient in that they did not go far enough to make a fundamental difference in the tiered nature of the system, nor far enough to resist a conservative retrenchment. Unfortunately, they made few substantial inroads on the rates of school failure. The record does not tell us that equality in education is a doomed cause, but that we have yet to try in a fully committed and comprehensive way.

To understand this dual character of liberal school reform, we offer an alternative reading of recent school history. Following World War II, there was a broad consensus in corporate, government, and public opinion that secondary education and, to some extent, higher education should become more widely accessible. The post-war expansion was moving into a new frontier of global and technological production, the government sector was mushrooming, the consumer economy called for a more developed service sector. These trends promoted a vast expansion of schooling and raised social minimums for literacy and for school duration. The high school diploma became the mass standard for school performance, serving both to elevate the general level of skill in the workforce and to ease job pressures by delaying the entry of youth into the labor market. Junior colleges and public universities proliferated; the GI Bill was the opening wedge of the modern school mission.

The upward mobility of organized workers and of the new white-collar middle strata also produced grassroots social pressure to broaden educational enfranchisement. Adequate schooling became as symbolic of the American Dream as the tract house in the suburbs; although not a root cause of the rising standard of living, educational attainment was one of its measures, a prized reward. The democratic and economic missions of schooling were indeed coinciding, and appeared to be converging. Significantly, the 1954 *Brown v. Board of Education* decision marked, for the first time, a formal commitment to include blacks in the promise of mobility.

## Egalitarian Demands

Through the 1960s, educational opportunities were greatly extended, particularly for the children of white workers in the primary labor force. But opportunities were still negligible, both in access and in resources, for the poor, for the marginal working class, and for minorities. The upsurge of the civil rights movement, reinforced by a mobilized student movement and by the progressive education tradition, raised challenges to these barriers. Demands for universal access to public education centered on the struggle for racial desegregation, but also called for the improvement of inner-city high schools, the expansion of community colleges, and admission to selective institutions. Resources to overcome social and educational disadvantages were demanded as well, including pre-school services, nutrition and social services, remediation, enrichment, and vocational programs.

From these initial struggles, a new vision of democratic education emerged, embryonic to be sure, but distinctly different from prior battles for inclusion. The reform movement questioned the basic construction of the school institution, its educational content, its classroom structures, and its forms of governance. From urban ghettoes to college campuses, the school reform movement sought more options and social relevance in the curriculum, alternative learning methods and environments, citizenship and empowerment skills, respect for cultural diversity. The movement sought schools that did not function as socioeconomic sorting mechanisms and did not assume that children failed because of individual or family deficits. The movement sought schools that operated with the expectation that all children could learn, given appropriate resources and flexible approaches. Integral to this call to transform the classroom was the vision of community control of decentralized school institutions, of parent advocacy and intervention, of student participation. The vision of democratic education was based neither on meritocracy nor on the lowest common denominator, but on a recognition that quality and equality must be measured by each other, that democracy must be taught by example.

It is easy, in these times, to underestimate the intensity of the egalitarian school reform movement of the '60s and early '70s. It should be recalled, however, that the school movement did not exist in isolation from other pressing social issues; it was a central part of the ferment for social justice that defined the political and cultural climate of that decade. The school movement drew on and developed within the activism of youth, minorities, women, the urban and rural poor. It was set in the context of confrontation in the Jim Crow South, of urban riots, of an unjust war, of Third World independence and women's liberation—a tide of social change and a moment of new expectations. And while the sharpest demands came from the angry poor and alienated young, there was a parallel impetus for more, if not different, educational opportunities among the ethnic working and middle classes.

The pressure exerted on schools, as central social institutions, did produce an unprecedented series of landmark legislation: the Vocational Education Act of 1963, and subsequent amendments, targeting low-income, handicapped, and female students; the Civil Rights Act of 1964, extending federal jurisdiction over equal opportunity; the Economic Opportunities Act of 1964, establishing the basis for community-based education and training programs; the Elementary and Secondary Education Act of 1965, the first broad federal support for public education, including Title I funding for compensatory education; the Bilingual Education Act of 1968 (ESEA Title VII), providing aid for bilingual programs; the Education Amendments Act of 1972 (ESEA Title IX), the federal bar on sex discrimination in school services; the Equal Educational Opportunity Act of 1974, mandating schools to redress language barriers; the Women's Educational Equity Act of 1974, funding women's studies; the Family Educational Rights and Privacy Act of 1974, assuring access to school records by parents and students; Public Law 94-142, the Education of All Handicapped Children Act of 1975, mandating a free, appropriate education to all handicapped children.

The period also produced significant court decisions, including *Mills v. D.C. Board of Education* (1972), establishing the access rights of handicapped children, and *Lau v. Nichols* (1974), mandating access rights for students with limited English proficiency. Desegregation plans were ordered; the right of undocumented immigrant children to public education was upheld; students' civil liberties were expanded; affirmative action was applied to school personnel. In addition, some school systems, particularly in urban areas, experimented with new approaches, introducing more socially relevant curricula, scrutinizing sex and race bias in texts, establishing alternative schools for drop-outs and students at risk. A large number of community colleges experimented with open admissions. Early childhood education programs were greatly extended in low-income communities, spearheaded by Head Start's pre-school program and the Follow Through program in primary grades.

Although the list of new government and school policies is impressively long, the reforms enacted still fell far short of the egalitarian demands that prompted them. These limitations stem both from flawed construction and from disabling implementation. The most important advance was enlarging access to public education for those previously disenfranchised, but inclusion was not matched by improvements in the quality of education provided to new entrants. Schools were indeed given new demands to meet, but these demands were not accompanied by either the level of resources or the institutional changes necessary to the task. Enrollments were broadened, but the educational ante was again raised, and the high school diploma or junior college certificate was devalued. Taken as a whole, the reforms of the '60s and '70s were cast in the classic pattern of extending inclusion while maintaining meritocratic structures of achievement.

The most significant potential challenge to the predictable outcome, school failure for the lower strata, was the enactment of categorical federal entitlement programs. The entitlement programs—Title I compensatory education, bilingual education, and special education for the handicapped—did represent more than legal access. They acknowledged that added resources were needed and that empowerment was an issue; each of the major entitlements originally included unprecedented mandates for parent advisory councils and intervention rights in the programs.

## Unkept Promises

Yet in their basic design, the entitlement programs were generally based on deficit assumptions about the inadequacies of minority students, rather than an assumption that the schools themselves were inadequate to an egalitarian mission. The models adopted were add-on programs, separate from rather than integrated with a reconstruction of mainstream schooling. The entitlements injected some urgently needed funding into distressed school systems; in many areas, they produced measurable gains for disadvantaged students. Where parent involvement was well developed, the entitlements have also produced a legacy of activism that remains influential well beyond school politics. But at the same time, the entitlement programs have worked within a tiered system to reinforce the segregation of students with special needs. Structurally, compensatory programs have established yet another basis for tracking, labeling, and lowered expectations.

If the reform design was a compromise, the implementation process has been a betrayal of egalitarian school demands, a record of unkept promises. Each of the major entitlements has been grossly underfunded, given the magnitude of services required to meet the needs of all children. In systems that face declining revenues and cutbacks in aid for regular programs, entitlement funds have frequently been treated as discretionary monies, and have been diverted from their original purposes. Many local school authorities have resisted responsibility for children who do not readily survive in the existing system, and have subverted mandates for parent involvement and approval. Non-compliance has not been systematically challenged by state and federal monitors. Often there are not enough qualified teachers, given low levels of compensation and poor training, to operate adequate programs.

In 1980, only 57% of the approximately 9 million students eligible for Title I were provided compensatory services, even though recent studies indicate the program has produced measurable gains for recipients. By 1982, it was estimated that Title I reductions had cut 900,000 children out of the program. In 1980, 77% of Hispanic children with limited English proficiency were not receiving any form of special programming responsive to their linguistic needs; only 10% were in bilingual programs. Special education students remain substantially underserved and overwhelmingly segregated. Vocational programs continue to practice wholesale sex discrimination, and the 30% cuts in federal funds for vocational education are a major setback for sex equity efforts. Even the most successful of all '60s programs, Head Start, which operates independently and innovatively with a record of unparalleled benefit for low-income children and their communities, today reaches only 18% of all eligible children.[3]

The history of desegregation offers an even more shameful example of rights denied through token policy commitments, feeble administration, and retreat in the face of regressive resistance. Although there are some laudable instances of successful desegregation—the NEA cites school systems in Seattle, Houston, and Charlotte-Mecklenburg[4]—the overall results thirty years after *Brown v. Board of Education* are deplorable. As of 1980, 63% of black children were attending predominantly minority schools.[5]

Jennifer Hochschild points out that most of the advances toward desegregation were achieved between 1968 and 1972, with no lessening of segregation since 1976.[6] Throughout much of the rural South, desegregation was accompanied by lowering the tax base for public schools, granting local and

state tax exemptions for segregation academies, and imposing what a Mississippi activist has called "martial law" by
local school boards.[7] Yet Hochschild reminds us that the
southern and border states have made the greatest advances
toward desegregation. "Racial isolation has increased considerably in the Northeast and is accelerating. As a consequence,
almost one-half of northern black students now attend all-
minority schools, compared to only one-quarter of southern black students. . . . [Moreover] resegregation or second-
generation discrimination within desegregated schools is
considerable."[8] In many areas of the country, desegregation
has coincided with cutbacks in school funding, opportunis-
tic polarizations of deprived whites and deprived minorities,
and the failure to raise school quality overall. The desegregation of districts has not necessarily produced desegregation
in local schools, in tracked programs within schools, or in
classroom placements. Today, our nation's schooling remains,
to a great extent, separate and unequal.

A large number of democratic demands have been aban-
doned altogether. Open admissions to public colleges lasted
less than five years, with little time, funding, or administrative support to establish viable transition programs. High
schools and colleges are increasingly dismantling their minority, ethnic, and women's studies programs. Decentralization of school governance was never achieved on any appre-
ciable scale; trends continue to favor the consolidation of
school districts, with even less influence by parents and
communities over local school policies and priorities. In addition, we have recently witnessed a growing divestiture of
federal and local taxpayer responsibility for public education, through cutbacks and tax revolts such as Proposition
13 and Proposition 2½. A recent study sponsored by the National Institute of Education (NIE) found that, with the con-

solidation of federal categorical funding under Chapter 2 block grants, there has been reduced assistance to urban schools, particularly those previously receiving desegregation aid, while federal aid to private schools has grown.[9]

What conservatives attack as corrosive egalitarianism never took place and is not the root cause of persistent school failure. The best of the '60s reforms have had marginal influence on school practice. The implementation process has been a shadow of the legislative intent, which was itself a shadow of popular demands for school equality. While conservatives justify the reversal of such reforms by claiming the programs did not work, they ignore the pervasive failure to make them work and the underlying social forces that have blocked a genuine commitment to progressive school change. Perhaps the most decisive factor has been prolonged economic stagnation, the pattern of recurring recession over the past fifteen years that has shifted national priorities away from social spending and equality goals.

In this climate of fiscal retrenchment, influential sectors of liberal opinion have retreated from their earlier alignment with social movements. In turn, those social movements have suffered serious setbacks and have become increasingly isolated, reducing the grassroots pressure on government. Another disabling factor has been the rising influence of school bureaucrats and professional organizations, which developed parallel to but increasingly apart from the grassroots mobilization for school change. These professional groups have tended to define their interests in opposition to community demands, seeking narrow control over the school institution and its traditional functions, frequently blocking the impetus for school reconstruction in order to maintain their own turf.

Each of these developments has opened the door for resurgent conservatism in school politics and for the reformulation of school goals along elitist lines. But to say that the egalitarian reforms of the '60s and '70s were denied the means to succeed is not to say that the attempt was not worth making. It is to say that the battle was far from won—we are still confronting the conflict between political democracy and economic elitism, between education as a tool of universal empowerment and education as a tool of selective mobility. We are still in a contest over extending the democratic potential of schooling or imposing the standard mold of meritocracy on new conditions.

What was gained by a decade of social activism was essentially a shift from exclusive meritocracy to inclusive meritocracy. Inclusion is not nothing, but it is not enough—and today, even formal access is eroding. Measures that recognized compensatory needs and addressed exclusion and segregation were real victories, but victories because they represented first steps toward more thorough institutional transformation. In the past ten years, those first steps have become inadequate and precarious. The task is now to match the inclusion of new populations in the schools with a new fully democratic mission for public education. Progressives won the first round and lost the second, but the vision that the '60s movement created survives to be built upon.

## 3. THE MYTH OF THE ECONOMIC IMPERATIVE

Before turning to the instructional and institutional approaches that serve a renewed vision of democratic education, it is important to examine a third myth that underpins the new elitism. This is the myth that we face an economic imperative to adopt get-tough prescriptions and competitive standards. The myth is based on the assumption that declining school performance is a major factor in declining economic performance. A corollary claim is that the restoration of high standards and discipline will help restore economic productivity, competitive advantage, and job creation. The elitisim of the new regime is thus justified by the claim that universal economic benefits will result.

We have argued that the fundamental crisis of education is not new, either in regard to massive failure to serve the bottom tiers or in regard to narrow concepts of achievement. This crisis does not correlate chronologically or causally with periods of economic decline. Furthermore, our reading of school history suggests that school performance has not been the motive force for economic growth. In fact, we find precisely the reverse dynamic at work: economic development has directed school change; economic status has determined school achievement; economic mobility has extended school opportunity. School functions have been largely subordinated to economic trends and, at most, play a supportive, not decisive role in the economy. And if schools have not shaped the economy in the past, they are even less likely to do so given current economic trends.

## The Economic Hourglass

For the past fifteen years, we have lived in an economy marked by stagnation, recurring recession, and the loss of international predominance. In the past five years, this economy has also gone through a period of dramatic restructuring, gearing up for a new round of global integration and intense competition. These conditions of prolonged contraction and structural change have accelerated the displacement of labor, so that today we face a shortage of jobs in a wide range of skill levels, not a shortage of qualified and motivated workers.

In October 1984, at the peak of a two-year "recovery" period, unemployment stood at 7.4%, or 8.5 million workers, a level that would have been considered recessionary twenty years ago. In addition, the index of "distressed workers"—which counts the discouraged who no longer look for work, the employed who remain in poverty, and involuntary part-time workers—stood at 14.2%, or 16.4 million people.[10] The figures for youth and for minorities are much worse. The jobless rate for black teenagers averages five times the national rate and today stands at well over 50%. Nearly 40% of the unemployed are under twenty-five years of age; nearly 20% are teenagers, who, in the recent upturn, garnered only 3% of all new jobs. Long-term trends indicate that the labor market will continue to contract relative to the workforce: the average jobless rate has risen steadily in each decade, from 4.2% in the 1950s, to 4.8% in the 1960s, to 6.2% in the 1970s, to 8.5% in the first four years of the 1980s.[11]

Structural shifts have also produced a sharper polarization of the workforce, a widening gap between skilled professionals and unskilled, low-wage service workers. We are witnessing the destruction of what for thirty years has been considered the primary workforce. The heart of that primary workforce has been blue-collar operatives in the leading industrial sectors—basic manufacturing, transportation, communications, construction. In general, these workers were unionized and received compensation tied to the rising productivity and the market advantages of their firms. Through the post-war period, this segment of the workforce set a pattern for wages, hours, and benefits, fair labor practices, and job security that became the pivotal standard for all American workers. Primary sector jobs were often semi-skilled and skilled, but educational attainment was not a major condition of job entry, training, or promotion.

These jobs are fast disappearing—over 5 million have been lost since 1980.[12] A once gradual erosion has become rapid and permanent displacement, due to several converging factors: the new wave of electronic automation, rising foreign competition, the flight of capital and production to cheap labor havens overseas, and the rise in non-productive investment. Job conditions are also worsening because of government deregulation of major industries (transportation, banking) and de facto deregulation of industrial standards (the gutting of EPA, OSHA, FDA, the NLRB). Union protections are rapidly weakening in the face of a new employer offensive, which for the first time since the formation of the CIO has held union wage gains below those of non-union workers.[13] The line between the primary and the secondary workforce is dissolving. The sector once reserved for low-skill, marginal, unorganized employment—and particularly for women and minorities—is now setting the pattern for job standards throughout the economy.

We confront a labor market with the middle dropping out and with competition growing at every level. Contrary to the human capital theories so optimistically put forward by current education influentials, there will not be more room at the top to compensate for the losses in the middle. The promise of high technology is not a workforce filled with technicians and skilled operatives; as a distinct sector, high-tech production will account for only 5–7% of job growth by 1990. Job growth is expected to occur in the service sector—in trade, finance, and personal services. A profile of the fastest-growing occupations of the decade shows that they are overwhelmingly low-skill and/or low-pay positions.[14]

TOP GROWTH OCCUPATIONS OF THE 1980S

| Occupation | Total Emp., 1981 (in 1,000s)* | Est. Increase, 1990 (in 1,000s) | % Female in 1981 | Average Weekly Wage in 1981 |
|---|---|---|---|---|
| All | 72,491 | 16,800 | 39.5 | $289 |
| 1. Secretaries | 3,199 | 700 | 99.3 | $230 |
| 2. Nurses' Aides | 832 | 508 | 84.3 | $172 |
| 3. Janitors | 993 | 501 | 14.6 | $219 |
| 4. Clerks (Sales) | 1,032 | 479 | 60.3 | $178 |
| 5. Cashiers | 712 | 452 | 85.1 | $227 |
| 6. Nurses | 1,168 | 438 | 95.8 | $332 |
| 7. Truckdrivers | 1,560 | 415 | 2.1 | $314 |
| 8. Fastfood | 1,000 | 400 | 50.9 | $171 |
| 9. Clerks (Office) | 2,082 | 378 | 76.2 | $201 |
| 10. Waiters | 532 | 360 | 85.1 | $150 |

* Full-time employees only.

In their enthusiasm for economic rationales, education policymakers have also widely ignored the displacement and deskilling effects of high technology on existing jobs. As Henry Levin and Russell Rumberger point out, the impact of new technology creates an initial increase in skill requirements, followed by a sharp and enduring decrease as mechanization proceeds. "Past applications of technology in the workplace, as well as the present evidence, suggest that future technologies will further simplify and routinize work tasks and reduce opportunities for worker individuality and judgment. Moreover, the displacement in jobs and the downgrading of skill requirements for most of the new positions will undermine employment generally, and especially the employment of skilled workers."[15]

The labor market of the future cannot be pictured as a bell-shaped curve, but rather as a bottom-heavy hourglass. The emerging top will include a small, elite strata of well-paid professional-technical employees, who themselves will face growing problems of skill devaluation and intense competition. The trend is already evident at the college level. Comparing jobs entered by college graduates from 1962 to 1969 with those entered from 1969 to 1978, the number of professional positions declined from 73.2% to 45.9%; the drop was taken up by sharp increases in clerical, sales, operative, service, and unemployed categories.[16]

On the bottom of the hourglass will be a shrinking number of blue-collar workers, faced with a continuous reduction of labor standards. The bottom will also include a growing segment of relatively skilled but low-paid employees in paraprofessional, technical, administrative, and service fields, a large proportion of them women. The bottom will include the traditional secondary workforce of low-skill, low-paid service jobs that are dead-end, unstable, and rapidly expanding. In addition, there will be a swelling pool of structurally unemployed workers, joining the vast reserve of irregular workers and hard-core unemployed.

## Designating the Victims

What labor market trends tell us is that a long-standing paradox of schooling will become a more intense contradiction in coming years: education will mean more for a few and less for many. Access to rewarding jobs will require greater educational attainment and proficiency, but there will be fewer chances of success even with the fullest schooling. For the great majority, job destinies will not utilize intellectual skills beyond basic literacy, although years of schooling may still count in arbitrarily sorting out who gets hired and who gets rejected. These trends suggest a series of problems we have just begun to grasp. Poor and minority youth, who already receive substandard schooling and face 50% unemployment, are likely to be left entirely outside the job market. Working class youth, who have no particular advantage in their schooling, will not have compensating job or income opportunities as adults. And schools will be increasingly hard-pressed to motivate their students through career aspirations or goals.

Given the disjuncture between economic and educational rewards, the effort to link school reform to the market value of education threatens to abandon large segments of American youth. If one argues that schools should reflect the logic of a polarizing labor market, the necessary conclusion is that we must reinforce competitive schooling—raise elitist barriers, add new stratification mechanisms, reward only the most exceptional or advantaged. Few other options are left within a marketplace framework. When public education was less than universal and the job market more expansive, it was still possible to add new, selective layers on top while opening up the bottom. But today it is harder to exercise the traditional option of creating differential values for schooling by extending its upper levels. The institution is filling up at all levels, and, even at the highest rungs, students are not finding economic status commensurate with their schooling.

Since the market can no longer be served by extending competition, the elitists would serve it by intensifying competition. The result of strictly meritocratic reforms will not be a better future for the majority, but new convenience in

55

designating the victims of both educational and economic deprivation. Today's get-tough policies work, in practice, as new ways to justify the enlargement of an underclass and the lowering of expectations for most others.

## THE SCHOOL-ECONOMY CONNECTION: FINDING NEW IMPERATIVES

The economic imperatives that are cited to defend competitive standards are actually compelling reasons for rejecting such standards. If the marketplace offers so many students diminishing rewards for education—and demands more punitive schooling in the process—we need to look beyond the marketplace in defining the school mission. This does not mean that schools should ignore the occupational futures that await their students, but that schools should be more forcefully egalitarian in light of employment inequalities. Further, school change should be linked to changing the marketplace itself, working to reorder economic priorities so that skill and knowledge are socially useful for every young person. In reformulating the connection of schools to the economy, we see three levels of needed reform.

### Democratizing Competition

The first challenge is to recognize that, within existing economic structures and polarities, there is a tremendous battle ahead simply to "democratize competition."[17] Even though job opportunities are limited, all children should have equal opportunities to succeed. Insistence on equity in access and in the quality of schooling will not transform the labor market, but equity can work to distribute labor market tyrannies more evenly. Although this represents only the minimum level of equal opportunity, we are far from fulfilling it. The focus today is on narrow forms of vocational training, with pressures for early tracking, test-driven and quantifiable curricula, and mastery of highly segmented and specific skills. School-to-work linkages, such as business partnerships and the federal JTPA program, are often only token efforts, frequently serving to cream the best students while neglecting the most needy.

To maximize their chances in a rapidly shifting and diversified job market, students need learning approaches that enhance their intellectual as well as vocational flexibility—a position firmly taken by the National Commission on Secondary Vocational Education, among others.[18] Students need schooling that emphasizes generic skills, reasoning capacity, and the social skills to interact with peers and teachers in tackling unfamiliar material. Schools also need to develop new approaches for economic literacy that go beyond instruction in filling out a job application or balancing a checkbook—students should have a realistic understanding of how the job market works and what barriers they will confront. Meaningful, paid work experience should accompany classroom training and be integrated with an academic program. Maximizing options also means challenging the rampant discrimination that prevails in vocational programs in the placement and instruction of female, minority, and low-income students. Along with affirmative action, there is an urgent need to address the counseling crisis in underfunded schools, particularly at the middle school level.

These are only some of the ingredients that could improve school-to-work linkages; the essential point is that the foundation for decent vocational preparation is a decent school, not just an extra program or a narrow skill. Deficient instruction, hostile school environments, attitudes of benign neglect based on low expectations are far more destructive than the absence of a computer science program, although computer science too should be demanded. Perhaps the basic priority is that we require schools to produce universal literacy—a feat nearly achieved by a number of very poor countries, far surpassing the United States, a very rich country that ranks 49th among 158 U.N. member nations in literacy.[19] Literacy is the minimal condition of labor market participation in tomorrow's economy, even in menial occupations, and it is the first order of failure in our schools.

## Restructuring the Economy

Beyond adjusting the school to the realities of the economy, a second challenge is to recognize a larger agenda for adjusting the economy to meet the needs of youth. Addressing this question involves the pursuit of a genuine national full employment policy, which accepts that where the private sector does not provide sufficient jobs, based on its market needs, then the public sector must provide jobs based on social needs. Across the country, chronic needs exist both for job creation and for rebuilding our communities. Viable models exist, both here and abroad, for public service employment and job training programs applied to infrastructural repair, environmental protection, social and family services, cultural activities, even schooling.

One of the more promising proposals, rejected by the Reagan administration but still on the congressional agenda, is the creation of a national youth service corps, directed to conservation and community service and modeled on the Civilian Conservation Corps (CCC). States and some cities are also pursuing this concept, which integrates public service employment with vocational training and academic remediation. In addition, major reforms of labor policy, incomes policy, and industrial policy can substantially affect job futures for youth. The long list of needed reforms includes measures to reduce the standard work week, regulate the export of capital, protect civil and union rights, establish pay equity, finance community development ventures, and enforce fair labor standards. The Catholic bishops have stressed the importance of a viable family wage to both reduce job pressures and provide parents more time for family and community sustenance;[20] even a liveable minimum wage would be a step forward.

Our comprehensive goals should not only establish the right to a job but, in the process, reconceive job structures and definitions of socially productive work. While these structural interventions in the national labor market are not on Washington's agenda—indeed, they are hostilely received by the present administration—they speak to conditions that this society will have to face in the coming decades. Economic polarization is damaging the social fabric and democratic potential of America at a dangerously accelerating pace; our failure to recognize this now will only make the task of adjustment and reconstruction more difficult and painful in the future.

The task of generating a national commitment to full employment, or even to extensive youth employment through the public sector, involves a long-term and highly political process that is not familiar territory for school activists. Educators themselves tend to draw strict lines between institutional and social politics, while at the same time despairing over how little impact internal school change has in the face of corrosive economic and social trends. Yet the school constituency can be a significant element in making the case for new economic priorities and in building citizen coalitions to reverse the present politics of corporate trickle-down. The new dynamism of state and urban politics, particularly the recent mobilization of minority electorates, represents an important opportunity to connect schooling needs to broader agendas for change and to initiate school-linked youth employment projects.

## Schooling for Citizenship

A third challenge posed by economic decline and school devaluation is to define the mission of education in terms of its citizenship function, rather than its labor market function. The current emphasis on competitive achievement, punitive discipline, and the segregation of diverse student populations, all work to reproduce societal modes of discrimination and cultural elitism. Emphasis on quantitative tasks, standardized and test-driven curricula, narrow skills acquisition—along with a notable lack of interactive learning environments—discourages students from thinking critically about their society and the choices confronting them. The isolation of schools from their communities further undermines the sense of civic responsibility and solidarity that public education should but rarely does cultivate among students.

The citizenship role of schooling, broadly conceived, addresses new imperatives of community life far more compelling—and more readily influenced by schools—than the demands of the economy. This society has undergone tremendous social transformation in the post-war period, which schools can respond to in both how they teach and what they teach. We have seen a long-term decline in voting and political participation. We have witnessed the devastation of older industrial and rural centers, increased crime and family violence, rising indicators of substance abuse and personal distress. We have a more mobile population that is also more multi-racial and multi-national. We have a rising percentage of older people and a more distinct youth subculture.

Probably the most dramatic changes are occurring in the status of women and in child-raising patterns. In 1980, 54% of children under eighteen had working mothers. The number of female-headed households has risen sharply; in 1980, 23.4% of all children under eighteen—17.3% of white children, 57.8% of black children—were not living in two-parent households.[21] Schools are serving a majority of children who do not come from "traditional" homes. Functions that we previously relied on the family to serve—including childcare, recreation, educational enrichment, cultural initiation, community involvement—are increasingly shifting to other social institutions, particularly schools.

In addition, the burdens of poverty in this society have fallen increasingly on women and children. Nearly 40% of all poor people in America are children. One in five American children is poor, one in two black children is poor, two in five Hispanic children are poor. Of adults in poverty, two out of three are women; nearly 50% of all female-headed households are poor.[22] There is a direct correlation of poverty to undereducation—not because poor children cannot learn, but because poor children go to poor schools. Our schools rarely do well if the traditional prerequisites for academic learning are not already in place, including parent literacy, adequate nutrition and healthcare, high self-esteem, and other social endowments.

Demographic studies tell us these trends will accelerate and that the school population of the future will be markedly different from that which schools have been organized

61

to serve in the past. There will be more children entering from poverty households and more poor children who do not get pre-school services, despite eligibility. There will be more children from single-parent households, more from families merged by remarriage, more "latchkey" children. There will be more children of teenage mothers, more children who were premature babies, more children whose parents were not married. And, if current practice holds, there will be more high school drop-outs and more college entrants who need both financial and academic assistance.[23]

Unfortunately, schoolpeople too often resent the added demands, blame underparenting or social problems for school failure, and ultimately disclaim responsibility for making the school culture more supportive of the child. New demands on schools to meet social needs are not the enemy of school achievement; in fact, meeting these needs is a condition for effective instruction and a key to raising levels of achievement. The issue is not the demands that are placed on schools, but the resources that are provided to help schools meet these demands.

Education for citizenship means that schools should provide children with the social and intellectual skills to function well as members of families and communities, as political participants, as adult learners, as self-directed individuals. Education for citizenship means teaching children about the way the world works and arming them to influence how it works. Citizenship requires basic skills, but it requires other forms of learning as well: critical judgment, social awareness, connection to community, shared values. The prescription is not more civics classes for seniors, although we should certainly upgrade civics instruction and civic experience. The priority is developing educational values that recognize all student needs as legitimate and that prepare students for multiple roles as adults, regardless of their labor market destinies or economic status. The bottom line for democratic education is empowerment, not simply employment. Indeed, an attempt to reduce the disjuncture between schooling and job futures will require an empowered citizenry that is prepared to reorder our economic priorities.

As we discuss alternative approaches for instructional and institutional change in the following sections of this book, we seek more than new formulas for skills proficiency and more than new mechanisms to distribute opportunity. We seek school improvement that will also promote the revaluation of education as a public institution—motivated by its ability to endow social knowledge and measured by its contribution to a more democratic and decent society.

# 4.

## School Practice: Ingredients of Effective Instruction

Elitist forms of meritocracy are not justified by the nature of the school crisis or the direction of economic development. Nor do they offer vehicles for effective schooling or school improvement. The neo-conservative prescription for change focuses narrowly on technical approaches and on reward-and-punish models of motivation. It confuses quantity with quality, calling for more uniformity, more promotional barriers, more tests, more homework, more time on task, more discipline. But the prescription does not explore the ways traditional school practice contributes to underachievement, or address the prospect that more of the same will simply compound the problem.

Moreover, the call for a tougher school regimen entraps the debate over change within a hard versus soft polarity, as if our choices are only more or less rigor, high or low standards, punitive or permissive incentives. We have noted that the case for hard approaches is often made by attacking the soft reformism of the '60s and '70s. Since equity reforms were so largely undermined in practice, since more children gained access without gaining quality schooling, the case has a superficial credibility. Since so many schools accommodated reform mandates by adding custodial rather than educational services, and even delivered such services in the name of social relevance or open education, these concepts have been easy to dismiss. Yet the failures of soft reformism do not justify the imposition of hard elitism. Both the hard and soft approaches arrive by different paths at low expectations for mass education, and both define equality as an issue distinct from excellence.

In discussing school change at the classroom level, it is important to resist such polarities and to understand the interrelation of factors that contribute to student achievement and school improvement. As we look at instructional approaches, however, we are mindful that attempts to reform how teachers and students function in school will require more than attention to the classroom or local school. As we argue in later chapters, progressive reform requires restructuring the constituent, governance, and funding processes that form the context for daily practice and determine the mission that schools serve. Nonetheless, the issues of how children learn and how teachers teach are both starting points and end points for school change. What we have learned about the ingredients of effective schooling establishes the concrete goals around which political and redistributive battles must be fought. Although it is not possible to address every important instructional issue in the scope of this book, we have focused on several topics that are central in the national debate and we suggest alternative ways to pose the issues.

## SETTING STANDARDS

### Curriculum: Content and Context

The achievement problem in American schools is twofold: there is an acute failure to endow low-income students with adequate basic skills, and a chronic failure to enhance all children's capacities to think critically and creatively. Both quantitative assessments, such as National Assessment of Educational Progress (NAEP) testing,[1] and qualitative studies, such as the work of Goodlad and Sizer, emphasize the need to stress cognitive development. Improving curriculum is one way to address the problem of both basic and higher-order skills, but neither the hard nor the soft poles of the debate offer useful solutions.

The hard approach currently prevails. The dominant thrust in recent state reform campaigns is to mandate some variety of "the one best curriculum" and to make course requirements more strenuous. By the latest count, at least forty-three states have increased the number of academic credits necessary for a high school diploma; thirty-two have changed curriculum standards or adopted new procedures for selecting textbooks.[2] Whether these programs use the label of core, basic, or universal, their goal is to expose all students to the same academic program and sequences. It is assumed that the core curriculum offers equal standards of quality and that all students have equal chances to succeed or fail. Few of these new mandates account for inequalities or even differences in student needs. Few acknowledge that schools themselves have unequal resources and different starting lines in the race to meet new requirements. Given the high failure rate with the curricula we now employ, imposing more rigorous requirements by legislative fiat will simply force more students to give up. It is tantamount to creating more obstacles in front of the hurdles many children have already failed to surmount.

Successful opposition to an elitist concept of standards must do more, however, than focus on the soft side of the polarity by arguing for a reduction of requirements. Reducing standards may or may not keep students in school, but lower standards will deny them the skills they need and will devalue their attainment. The real alternative to tougher curriculum is better curriculum, which stresses multiple approaches. Students should have thorough exposure to the core of basic skills, but they should also have a curriculum that is relevant to their social environment, that develops creative and interpretive skills, and that recognizes cultural diversity as a resource, not a deficit, in learning. The issue is not more or less math or science, but making each subject more useful and challenging to the student—and addressing why the subject has not been engaging to those who fail it. There should be common standards, but flexibility in the pedagogies and sequences used to meet them.

Where curriculum and mastery requirements are legislated, this flexibility and diversity is almost always preempted. In the process of imposing instructional mandates, we also lose sight of the limited impact curriculum has as a discrete factor in achievement. A growing body of research points to the interrelation of many ingredients in determining school performance. These ingredients are generally qualitative—the level of expectations, the degree of collaboration, the opportunity for innovation, the extent of participatory decision-making. They add up to a particular school culture within which a range of curricular or pedagogical approaches can succeed. Effective Schools research has identified a number of schools that produce high achievement levels for disadvantaged students, and the difference between these and schools that perform poorly is not the mandated curriculum, or the composition of the student body, but the character of the total school environment.

A report by the Ford Foundation's High Schools Recognition Program (1981–83) identifies the pattern associated with school improvement in 300 public high schools, based on research and on-site observation. The schools were selected for achieving significant improvements in overall student performance; they were large, urban schools, with predominantly low-income, minority students. Among the internal forces for positive change, observers found "school-based leadership, . . . a stable, versatile and cooperative faculty and staff, . . . and consensus within the school about standards for discipline, attendance, and expectations for students and teachers."[3]

More specifically, the Ford report observes that in each school, staff recognized that they were expected to serve all students equitably. School management practices allowed vigorous leadership by principals, teachers, counselors, and other staff; often strong parental and community involvement was developed. Many schools developed solid working relationships with outside support groups, including adult volunteers, student tutors, area employers, community-based social service agencies, and local colleges and universities. Schools initiated new teaching and learning programs in basic skills and academic subjects. Factors that contributed to sustained progress included: a team approach among faculty and support staff; ongoing in-service staff and leadership development programs; clear and simple standards for student behavior designed with student and parent participation; additional, discretionary funds for instructional initiatives; and district support or acquiescence in the development of more flexible instruction and planning.

Among the problems that impeded improvement, the report cites decaying facilities, student turnover, and the high incidence of students in need of supportive academic and social services. More disabling, however, were the limited resources available to the schools due to funding cutbacks—especially in compensatory, bilingual, and special education—as well as chronic underfunding of teacher development and in-service training programs. Moreover, the Ford report finds:

> The current emphasis on minimum basic skills, with mandated curricula and methods of teaching and testing, has narrowed the scope of education for some students. Often, too, these mandated programs underuse teachers' abilities and, worse, neglect the development of students' ability to think, analyze, and inquire. In some schools, the basic skills "floor" had become the "ceiling" of achievement.[4]

The Ford report confirms similar conclusions reached in Effective Schools research, a range of school improvement projects in recent years, and the experience of alternative high schools designed for students at risk.[5] These practical efforts have demonstrated repeatedly that quality schooling produces solid achievement for poor and minority students, and that the key is restructuring the total school environment. As Stewart Purkey and Marshall Smith comment, in a review of Effective Schools research:

> Reforms that fragment the instructional program or that treat only one aspect of the school social system are likely to leave untouched the school's culture. They may also diminish teachers' sense of responsibility for what happens to the students

and the school as a whole, since only certain parts of the school are diagnosed as needing improvement. . . . This sense of diminished responsibility may also result from the imposition of other piecemeal educational panaceas such as "teacher-proof curriculum" and scripted instructional technologies. Whatever the merit of such innovations, their prescriptiveness and particularly their dictated use may actually erode teachers' willingness to accept responsibility for student success. The academic developers blame teachers for not correctly using the package, and teachers blame the technique for being inappropriate, while the core of the problem may lie in an organizational structure that attempts to impose one best cure-all from the top down.[6]

## Time: Quantity and Quality

A parallel argument applies to the current debate over school time. Most prominent national reports stressed an urgent need for more time on task, more time in school, a longer school day, and a longer school year. The reports relied heavily on the dubious examples of Japanese and European systems, which are far more rote and elitist than our own. Again, a more/less time polarity creates a false issue; what is at stake is not the quantity but the quality of learning time in our classrooms.

John Goodlad, for example, painstakingly demonstrates that 95% of classroom time is dominated by teacher talk. Extending this one-dimensional pedagogy is likely to increase rather than relieve the mutual demoralization of teachers and students. Traditionalists have ignored quality-time issues, but there are alternative approaches. Educators are developing an increasingly sophisticated understanding of how effective classrooms work. The evidence appears in a growing body of recent work, including classroom studies by Goodlad, Sizer, Brophy, Rosenshine, Good and Grouws, Denham and Lieberman, and the California Beginning Teacher Evaluation Study.[7] We can also draw upon the experience of various open classroom models, and experiments developed under Title I compensatory education programs. The pedagogical elements of effective classrooms include: reducing teacher isolation through practices like team teaching; increasing teacher-student interaction; increasing student initiative and peer interaction through peer teaching and mentor programs. Teacher-directed curricula, supported by teacher-directed in-service training, appear to be positive factors as well.

There is also convincing evidence for restructuring the organization of time that our schools so rigidly and pervasively follow: the forty-five to fifty minute periods in secondary school and the scheduling of discrete subjects in short blocks across the school day. Underlying these time practices are the assumptions that repetition is the key to learning, that student concentration is a matter of discipline, and that all children should be programmed to progress at uniform rates. Alternative approaches indicate the value of variable time, of longer segments that increase the opportunity for more personal student-teacher relations, of segments that combine subjects in an interdisciplinary approach, and of sequences developed according to the student's learning pattern and progress.[8] Successful alternative education programs for drop-outs and adults also suggest that we need to be more flexible in the age structure of schooling to allow access to public schooling across each student's lifetime. Free high school is a universal entitlement for youth only until their eighteenth year, but high school could be made available to students at any age, based on their own readiness and priorities, with far less stigma and penalty for not following the set pattern.

Finally, an obvious way to increase effective learning time, *reducing class size*, is ignored by all the recent commission reports. Yet with ratios of thirty-five or forty to one in many urban classrooms, individual students cannot get the attention they need and teachers have little incentive or means to encourage personalized instruction. If more is better, why not create more teacher time for each student, instead of extending mandatory attendance in overcrowded classrooms? Reducing class size requires money, but so does a longer school day or year. The time issue, in all its dimensions, is not simply one of resources, given the appalling waste of teacher and student energies we currently foster in a rigidly time-bound and lockstep system. The issue is one of narrow vision and limited objectives for what constitutes achievement and who should achieve.

## Assessment and Testing

The use of standardized testing as the primary assessment tool in public schools is one of the most controversial issues of the current school debate. Conservatives generally support extensive testing and the use of test scores to determine tracking, promotion, graduation, and credentialing. Progressives often point out the abuses involved in standardized testing, but appear divided on their usefulness. What is clear, however, is that standardized testing is rapidly expanding throughout education as the one best measure of achievement. Most states now require students to pass some form of basic skills proficiency test in order to graduate, and many are extending these testing "gates" into elementary grades.

An extreme example of the trend is Minneapolis' new requirement that kindergarten children pass a skills test determining whether they are held back or allowed to enter first grade.

There is a wealth of research that indicates the glaring, even damaging, limitations in the ways schools use norm-referenced standardized tests.[9] The indictment includes issues that are deeply significant to our democratic commitments in education. First, standardized tests have been shown to be culturally biased in ways that consistently discriminate against minorities and non-middle class students; some have suggested they are more accurate as a measure of the out-of-school effects of student experience than the in-school effects.[10] Second, the statistical procedures used to set standards are dictated by the bell-shaped curve, which gives us a rank order of students, without indicating the actual level of mastery achieved. Third, the tests do not measure a wide range of capacities and qualitative skills, but measure how well students take time-restricted, machine-scored multiple choice tests. Fourth, test results are increasingly used as punitive mechanisms against both students and teachers, as the basis for labeling, tracking, demotion, promotion, exclusion.

Fifth, as Deborah Meier has persuasively argued, standardized testing increasingly erodes curriculum and subordinates teaching.[11] We are in danger of developing a singularly test-driven system of education. Students are encouraged to narrow their acquisition of knowledge to the atomized information that is test-effective. Teachers are encouraged to gear instruction to test performance, to vie for the most test-responsive students, and to study the pedagogy of successful test-taking. Administrators are encouraged to manipulate the results and, by many accounts, frequently do. If the crisis of excellence in education is centered on our failure to promote higher-order reasoning and critical thinking, over-reliance on standardized testing will promote this deficiency.

At the same time, any critique must consider that standardized testing is at present the major instrument for making performance comparisons over time and between programs and has become a major tool for public accountability. The concern about measuring school performance in tangible ways is legitimate. Parents of poor and minority students, who suffer the most harmful consequences of test bias, often call for standardized testing as an attempt to guarantee that their children's academic proficiency will be assessed and advanced. In some cases, tests have been demanded to guard against biases in subjective evaluation. Standardized testing has usefully confirmed the gains achieved by programs like Head Start, Follow Through, and Title I.

The crux of our critique is that standardized testing is not simply applied to comparisons of school performance, or program outcomes, but that it is used to designate *student* failure to meet often arbitrary standards. If standardized testing were considered primarily a diagnostic tool for teaching, one of several instruments used to identify effective or ineffective classrooms and programs, its limitations would not be so serious or irremediable. But in school systems throughout the country, standardized testing is inappropriately used to regulate student placement and progress and to reward or punish individual students and teachers. In this context, test scores are not diagnostic, but prescriptive and punitive; their limitations as measures of achievement and their misuse as measures of potential become damaging. Poor test scores can amount to life sentences for students, another form of self-fulfilling prophecy that produces school failure or underachievement.

An alternative approach to the testing dilemma is to develop a variety of assessment instruments for both student and school performance. Assessments that are more reflective of overall student capacity include joint teacher and parent evaluations, criterion-referenced testing, and indicators of progress in meeting individualized learning goals. Standardized testing may have appropriate uses in comparatively assessing groups of students across classrooms, grade levels, and schools. But other indices of instructional performance must be considered as well, including peer evaluations among teachers, quality-of-school-life scales, progress in meeting school improvement objectives, attendance and drop-out rates, promotion and retention rates.

Testing itself is not the core issue. The issues are whether the test used is valid for what it purports to measure; whether the test assesses performance or dictates performance; whether the results are used to correct instructional deficiencies or to stratify students. By these criteria, we have ample reason to challenge the extraordinary legitimacy now vested in standardized testing and competitive test scores.

## TEACHING SUPPORT SYSTEMS

A central focus of all the national reports and current legislative reform programs is the need to upgrade teacher quality. Some of these efforts assume there has been massive deterioration in teacher competence, a notion based on the declining SAT scores of teaching candidates. Other kinds of data do not indicate a sharp decline; one study shows a steady increase in the percentage of appropriately credentialed teachers now in the schools.[12] While the competency issue remains highly disputed, there is no doubt that a crisis in

75

professional and workplace conditions exists and has created serious problems for recruiting, retaining, and sustaining an effective teaching corps.

In the policy arena, the greatest attention has been paid to factors such as low pay, poor preparation, limited career mobility, and lack of prestige. The most popular response has been to institute merit pay systems, master teacher programs, and competency testing, along with revising certification requirements. In many cases, the approach is more punitive than supportive, assuming that meritocratic mechanisms for designating success and failure are sufficient prods to quality. This is particularly the case with formulations of merit pay that reward only the "best" and punish the "worst," using dubious methods of assessment and leaving the vast middle range of teachers unaffected, as well as disaffected. A recent study by the Association for Supervision and Curriculum Development, for example, reports that many newly instituted merit pay systems are proving counter-productive. The study found that these merit systems were difficult to administer, produced hostility among teachers, reduced the capacity of supervisors to offer qualitative evaluations, and undermined collaborative relations between teachers and administrators.[13] The resort to competency testing is as problematic for teachers as it is for students, since some of the most critical attributes of good teaching cannot be measured by standardized, quantitative procedures.

While confrontations over merit pay and competency testing have captured the headlines, recent reform efforts have also stimulated proposals that stress professional development and collective support mechanisms. There has been widespread recognition of the need to increase base salaries, which now average $15,400 nationally, the lowest of any profession. The concept of establishing innovative career ladders, which allow teachers multiple roles and responsibilities during their careers, has become widely accepted, if not widely implemented. Congress and some states are establishing scholarships to encourage more qualified entrants, especially in the high-shortage areas of science, math, and special education. Growing attention is being given to the long-standing deficiencies of professional education, which has emphasized classroom management techniques more than academic preparation or child development training. At the same time, there is concern that pedagogical training will be needlessly sacrificed to academic concentrations, at a moment when educational methodology is improving and can truly contribute to classroom performance.[14]

Teachers need higher pay and more opportunities for reward and advancement. Yet the focus on pay and career incentives will not achieve much if policy-makers overlook some of the more fundamental questions about teaching conditions that have demoralized the profession. Teachers' lives are structured not only by terms of employment but by the size of their classes, by their isolation in the classroom, by inadequate time for study and planning, by the neglect of practical training, by competitive and atomizing performance measures, by standardized and test-driven curriculum designs, by pedagogical directives and "teacher-proof" curricula that reduce the teacher to technician, and by hierarchic and autocratic governance systems. For a profession that has the potential for high personal rewards, teaching under these conditions is bound to generate disappointment and more than likely to produce the cynical defensiveness so characteristic of teacher burn-out.

The point is underscored by studies that show that teachers feel trapped by their impotence in changing the quality of education as much as by the lack of advancement opportunity.[15] Research on teacher effectiveness shows no correlation between teacher salary and student achievement.[16] The critical correlates that distinguish the staffs of effective schools are that these staffs have high expectations for all students and low turnover. No specific pedagogy and no one set of teacher rewards has been linked to high expectations or staff stability—once again, the decisive ingredients are qualitative conditions of school climate and organization. To generate teacher initiative and liberate their expectations, we must provide more comprehensive support systems *and* restructure the hierarchic school management structures that frustrate the performance of so many teachers.

Teacher support programs need to include a much stronger emphasis on staff development that is teacher directed, that includes mentor systems, and that counts as part of the workload. The national movement to develop local teacher centers offers a variety of positive models. Teachers also need more time that is not tied to classroom management. They need time both to give individualized attention to students and to enhance their own skills through study, curriculum development, and program evaluation. Teachers need autonomy, the space and responsibility to exercise professional judgment and to creatively adapt the school program to student needs. Teachers need accountability methods that utilize peer-assessment and that provide resources for overcoming deficiencies.

Equally important is the reform of school management practices to create more collaboratively run schools. A number of models exist from open classroom experiences and alternative schools that show the benefit of cooperative planning, team teaching, reciprocal observation, peer training, and teacher-based school improvement projects. Some programs, like the original Title I, also involve parents and para-professionals in team-teaching and planning. School-based management experiments in California, South Carolina, and Florida, as well as numerous local districts, have included teachers in joint governance councils that make significant decisions about school policy, the use of discretionary funds, and program implementation. School improvement projects based on Effective Schools research generally make inclusive decision-making at the local school level a primary objective. In later chapters, we will return to matters of management and governance, along with the role of the unions, but the issue of teacher participation is not merely a formal democratic one. Collective power-sharing in school management is a condition for engaged and responsive teaching.

Using these models to begin restructuring our schools is a complex and difficult task. But to ignore the task by devising merit pay schemes or new tests is to play the traditional game of school reform—discovering solutions that avoid the problem. If we tinker with teaching to make it more merit-ocratic, but fail to meet teachers' critical needs for collaboration and development, a few individual teachers may feel honored, but many more will continue to feel entrapped.

To change the experience of teaching, we cannot simply transform our teachers. On the most pragmatic grounds, it appears there will be a shortage of teachers by 1990, due largely to poor pay and working conditions, which will work against a more exclusive and more selective approach to up-grading the profession.[17] But meritocracy also misses the strategic point: to change the experience of teaching, we must change the teaching environment; to change the status of teaching, we must revalue the institution in which teachers work.

## ENTITLEMENT PROGRAMS

With the conservative shift in the national political climate has come a direct assault on federal entitlement programs for compensatory, bilingual, and special education. These programs have been at the core of efforts to redress the long-standing inequities of our school system and to improve access to quality education for low-income and special needs students. These entitlements are now facing crippling funding cutbacks and a persistent campaign to discredit their intent as well as their practice. The defense of entitlements is thus a critical battle in repudiating the new elitism in education. Yet as we discussed in our review of '60s school history, the entitlement programs do not represent unflawed reforms.

The entitlements responded to intense social pressure from minorities and the urban poor, who demanded federal responsibility not only for enlarging equal opportunity but for promoting equality of results for groups that had been traditionally victimized by racism, exclusion, and second-class schooling. The entitlements did not live up to these demands. They went beyond previous access and inclusion reforms by offering compensatory categorical programs, and they injected some urgently needed funding into distressed districts. But the entitlements were designed as adjunct services that left the existing structures of schooling unchallenged. The add-on approach derived from the assumption that children at risk are deficient and did not address the concept that schools are inadequate to meet their needs. This debilitating compromise in design was followed by an even more crippling implementation process. Through chronic underfunding of both categorical and mainstream programs, through administrative subversion, and through negligence in enforcing student and parent rights, the entitlement programs have failed to reach or appropriately serve the majority of students they target. In some cases, they have become new mechanisms for stigmatizing and segregating children, generating a new bottom tier in schooling for the masses.

Despite these compromises, the entitlement programs achieved some real successes. Where commitments to equity goals were sustained, specific programs developed valuable models for program innovation, needs assessment, and parent participation. Further, both the successes and failures have taught us something about new conditions that are necessary, along with adequate funding, to make entitlements for categorical need effective. Fundamentally, those conditions involve vast improvements in the mainstream of education to accommodate a diversity of individual needs, to increase teaching resources, and to allow flexible program design.

The best defense of entitlement programs involves: (1) upholding the original premise that government has responsibility to fund education according to children's needs; (2) ensuring that the entitlements are funded and monitored to serve all eligible children; (3) restoring and extending the mandates for parent participation; (4) requiring that improvements in categorical services be integrally linked to inclusive reforms in mainstream education and linked to campaigns for overall school improvement.

## Compensatory Education

The most successful school entitlement has been compensatory education, first enacted as Title I under the 1965 Elementary and Secondary Education Act (ESEA) and supplemented by a number of state compensatory programs. De-

spite the conservative assertion that compensatory education has negligible impact and primarily promotes minority
patronage, recent NAEP assessments and SAT scores indicate
real, if modest, gains in narrowing the gap between minority
and white student achievement, which many attribute to
the cumulative effects of Title I remedial services.[18]

Compensatory programs vary considerably, and many demonstrate all the limitations cited above in regard to segre-
gative and deficit models. However, Title I did generate programs that transcended deficit assumptions and broke new
ground in effective education practice. Teachers and aides
hired by Title I programs were often more representative of
poor and minority communities, more attuned to student
need, and more willing to test new approaches. The Title I
mandate for parent participation through advisory councils
has trained and motivated a generation of school activists in
a number of urban and rural districts, from New York to Mississippi. These activists have become an enduring source of
leadership for numerous advocacy and community action
organizations.

In addition, the relative freedom of compensatory programs fostered a range of teaching innovations that are of
value not only in remedial classes but in regular classroom
settings as well. Title I spurred the development of new reading and math programs, coupled with new teaching styles
such as peer tutoring, learning games, small-group and individualized instruction. Schoolwide programs that integrate
compensatory programs with regular education have successfully lowered class size, pioneered the use of paraprofessionals, and reduced the divisions between mainstream and
special staff. Compensatory education's focus on assessing
need and designing specific need-based programs has been

adopted by many districts as the basis of effective curriculum planning.

The original Title I has now become watered down into Chapter 1 of the Educational Consolidation and Improvement Act. The Reagan administration has severely weakened the parent participation mandate, but its attempt to gut Chapter 1 aid was met by concerted national resistance that saved approximately 60% of previous funding. Since state-funded compensatory programs have not made up the shortfall, disadvantaged students with basic skills needs are receiving significantly less remedial help than they received over the past two decades. The Children's Defense Fund indicates that as many as 900,000 students lost Title I services. In addition, thirteen states have entirely eliminated specific Title I/Chapter 1 programs, including math and pre-school programs.[19] Despite these grave setbacks, the record of compensatory education has at least shown us that entitlements are a terrain worth defending.

## Bilingual Education

The current conservative onslaught against bilingual education is tempered only by partisan contention for Hispanic voters, who overwhelmingly support bilingual education programs. Attacks against bilingual education start from the claim that it does not work, a theme recently taken up by Secretary of Education William Bennett. In several public statements during 1985, Bennett cited the persistence of low achievement and high drop-out rates among Hispanic students as confirmation that bilingual programs are failing and no longer merit federal investment. He did not add, however, how minimal that investment has been and the fact that the vast majority of eligible students receive no English language assistance whatsoever—facts that suggest quite opposite conclusions about why Hispanic students are not catching up.

The effort to discredit bilingual education also has its xenophobic elements. The Twentieth Century Fund Task Force on Education, for instance, insists that schools' "failure to recognize the primacy of English is a grave error" and recommends that federally funded programs eliminate instruction in students' native languages.[20] The Far Right proposes a constitutional amendment that would make English the exclusive official language of the United States.

The defense of bilingual education must begin with the recognition that both federal statute and the Supreme Court have declared that children of national minority groups with limited English proficiency (LEP) are entitled to an equal education in a language they can understand. In 1974, the Supreme Court's *Lau v. Nichols* decision declared that school districts must take affirmative steps to make education accessible to these children and that mastery of English cannot be a precondition for access to education. While the Court was not asked to prescribe a specific remedy, it noted that bilingual education was a way for districts to meet their responsibility and upheld federal remedies that promoted bilingual education. Subsequently, the federal government— and many state legislatures—have formally favored bilingual education as the most comprehensive option to provide children with access to schooling as they learn English.

However, despite the *Lau* decision and ten years of federal law, two-thirds of the nation's LEP students still do not receive *any* type of special language services—not bilingual education, not special instruction in English.[21] Under the Bilingual Education Act of 1968, ESEA Title VII, the federal government has provided relatively little funding to districts that choose to implement bilingual programs. Moreover, Title VII defines bilingual education fairly loosely, as a program that provides instruction in English and uses the child's native language "to the extent necessary to allow a child to achieve competence in the English language." The statute leaves the scope and amount of use of the native language open to the local district, resulting in a wide variety of programs that qualify as bilingual education. The most comprehensive, but least utilized, bilingual approach emphasizes maintenance of the native language alongside the mastery of English; such programs often include a bicultural curriculum and stress the integrity of national heritage. By far the more common bilingual approach is the transitional program, which typically uses the child's native language for 25% or less of instructional time and discontinues its use as soon as possible. In 1980, it was estimated that only 10% of Hispanic children with limited English proficiency were in either type of bilingual program.[22]

Most frequently, schools have responded to legal mandates with non-bilingual special programs, such as English as a Second Language (ESL) or structured "immersion" programs, which teach English without recourse to the native language. This approach is particularly favored in schools where there is a shortage of bilingual teachers, where there are small numbers of LEP students, or where LEP students come from a variety of language backgrounds. When properly designed and adequately funded, some of these programs produce basic mastery of English. But too often the advocates of English immersion are really promoting the traditional "sink or swim" approach, through poorly conceived, understaffed, and underfunded programs. It is the rule, not the exception, that hostility to bilingual education among schoolpeople, combined with meager federal funding, has produced programs that caricature federal mandates and predictably fail LEP students.

Yet sufficient evidence exists that native language teaching aids the acquisition of English and that total immersion is not the most effective method.[23] Forced assimilation, along with programs that hold students out of mainstream academic curricula until they learn English, are needlessly retarding and humiliating. Moreover, we consistently deny bilingualism as a resource in the language education of all students, when bilingual programs could well be reciprocal with mainstream curriculum. In a collaborative school environment, bilingual education could help all students acquire linguistic skills and multi-cultural exposure, both as peer-tutors and as second-language learners. It is a troubling paradox that many states are currently imposing foreign language requirements for high school graduation and college entrance, while stripping non-English speaking minorities of their bilingual capabilities and cultural dignity at an early age.

Due to pressure from bilingual educators and the Hispanic community, Congress has recently confronted the polarization over bilingual education and rewritten Title VII. The new act recognizes that high-caliber bilingual programs continue to provide the best educational opportunity for most LEP students. Accordingly, the bulk of funds are reserved for transitional bilingual programs. The new law also strengthens these programs by upgrading teacher training and retraining efforts and by improving evaluation and monitoring criteria. In addition, several new demonstration programs are authorized. Developmental Bilingual Education programs respond to the need to develop language resources for all students, by creating integrated programs where children of any

language background can learn two languages. The new provision for Special Alternative Instruction addresses the need
for better all-English programs where schools have multi-
lingual populations or where communities prefer this approach. The intent is to ensure that non-bilingual programs
are carefully designed, appropriately staffed, and adequately
funded. Parental choice and participation are also increased
in the new Title VII legislation.

The 1984 legislation represents an improvement in program options and accountability and a setback for the conservatives who sought to eliminate native language instruction, restrict eligibility, shorten the duration of services, and
further cut Title VII funding. But bilingual education still
faces serious challenges, including budget freezes and hostility at the state level. Federal funds support and influence
only a small portion of bilingual or special English instruction programs. The entitlement exists in law, but clearly has
far to go in practice, when only one-third of children with
limited English proficiency are receiving language assistance
and most of these remain in programs that offer little better
than "sink or swim."

## Special Education

The passage of Public Law 94-142 in 1975 guaranteed to all
students with handicapping conditions the right to an appropriate education in the least restrictive environment. Federal
administrative codes and state regulations have translated
this act into local practice that is always complex, often
costly, and at times inflexible. In many parts of the country,
especially rural areas, virtually no initiative has been taken
by school authorities to develop their district's special education capacities, and parents are faced with difficult battles

over non-compliance. In areas where compliance is pursued, the severe underfunding of both special and regular education has often created damaging trade-offs between different types of need, pitting the needs of children with handicapping conditions against the needs of children in the mainstream.

There is also considerable documentation of classification abuse, which turns the increasingly segregated special education system into a dumping ground for "hard-to-teach" children or students with discipline problems. Statistics compiled by the U.S. Department of Education's Office of Civil Rights indicate that, in some categories, referrals to special education classes are becoming more and more discriminatory, removing disproportionate numbers of minority and poor students from mainstream classrooms.[24] Ironically, misclassification may also be encouraged by the fact that special education classes are generally smaller, with higher staffing ratios—parents or staff may be persuaded that a child will have a better chance in a special ed class, even when that class is not designed to meet that student's particular problem in school. Both current regulations and funding mechanisms foster the removal of children from regular schooling, rather than the adaptation of the mainstream to a wider range of needs. To reverse the pattern requires a commitment to provide mainstream classrooms with the staffing, guidance, and training support that teachers require to be effective with diverse student populations.

We cannot return to past conditions in which schools excluded special needs students, took no responsibility for their education, or placed them in restricted environments. But we cannot defend special education on the basis of the present debilitating conflicts in how it is implemented. The key to making special education function adequately lies as much, if not more, in the reform of the mainstream as it does in combating its present abuses. Such reform should include extending the concept of individualized education programs (IEPs), now mandated in special education, to all students—as the basis of both equalizing and distinguishing the complete spectrum of needs they present.

## NEW APPROACHES TO INSTRUCTIONAL PRACTICE

There are, of course, many other issues that are central to improved instruction. Tracking as a stratification mechanism certainly warrants a full critique, particularly in light of research on the effectiveness of peer teaching among heterogeneous student groups.[25] Discipline is an important issue, which again should be reviewed outside the usual hard/soft polarity, in light of the effectiveness of participatory school management. Drop-out prevention is another crucial topic—the experiences of alternative schools and high-support programs indicate successful approaches that could be applied in the restructuring of elementary as well as high school practices.

Given the survey nature of this report, we have limited our arguments to curriculum, time, testing, teacher support, and categorical programs. But these topics raise points that are useful in evaluating all aspects of instructional reform. First, it seems abundantly clear that no one or two elements of the school program can transform school performance. Each element should be viewed in terms of its interaction with the total school and seen as a leverage point rather than an end point for change. Quantitative approaches cannot substitute for qualitative change. Technical prescriptions do not address the teaching and learning processes, which are conducted through relationships operating within distinct social environments. Similarly, top-down approaches, imposed prescriptions, and narrow mandates are more likely to generate defensive resistance than to liberate the energies of school staff, especially when supportive resources do not accompany new requirements.

Second, the discussion points to a fundamental reciprocity between the task of achieving equality for students who are now grossly underserved and the task of enhancing the intellectual capacities of all students. The ingredients of school improvement for the most distressed schools are also ingredients for making all schools more engaging, more attuned to individual potential, more collectively supportive. We have also noted that there are useful models to be drawn from categorical programs—from Title I and, even more, from the Head Start and Follow Through programs. And if improving services to students with special needs depends ultimately on reforming the mainstream, such reform can also enlarge the school's responsiveness to all students. Conversely, the advantages enjoyed in privileged schools, public and private, can be universalized for all schools: smaller class size, tutoring and personal counseling, extracurricular trips and programs, parent consultation, to name a few.

Finally, the discussion underlines the point that inadequate schooling is not essentially a problem of techniques, but of commitments. There is a rich and growing body of research, observation, and experience in education on approaches that stimulate effective instruction; as one commentator put it, "a scientific basis is finally emerging for the art of teaching."[26] Though scarcely without controversy, the field is presenting a more complex understanding of the learning process and the organizational dynamics of schooling than today's quick-fix reforms acknowledge. New approaches, techniques, programs, models are available to get us beyond the limits of traditional schooling and the traditional schizophrenia over elite versus mass education. The question arises: if we can identify the ingredients of successful schooling, using uncompromised standards of both excellence and equality, why can't we direct the reform process to deal with the qualitative issues of school change? Certainly, the critique raised here is represented by many articulate voices in the academic debate. But the direction of further reform will depend less on what educational research presents than on whose interests and social vision prevail in the institutional and political arenas of power.

# 5.

# School Constituents: Directions for Change

We have argued that improving instruction for all students involves creating more supportive, flexible, and collaborative school environments and enlarging the commitment to equality of results. Achieving these improvements is primarily a matter of political choices and priorities rather than a problem of technique. This political context of school change raises a new set of questions: Who are the constituencies of democratic school reform? How can they be activated to change the balance of power in school management and policy? What structural school conditions support their involvement?

The issues of institutional politics do not emerge easily from the current school debate, which has tended to narrow the focus to the immediate classroom arena and to a quest for "good schoolpeople." This narrow focus leaves the larger political field to entrenched bureaucratic interests and conservative forces, who already wield considerable power in setting the school policy agenda and who prefer meritocratic school regimes to democratic approaches that might raise expectations or shift school authority. To challenge the institutional arrangements of schooling it is therefore necessary to go beyond the politics of instruction. The history of education repeatedly warns us that when reform efforts ignore issues of institutional power, they are ultimately resisted, co-opted, or fragmented.

The crisis in public schools will not be effectively or fairly addressed without constituent participation in the change process. The frontline constituencies of education are parents, students, classroom teachers, support staff, local school administrators, and community members, including youth and education advocacy groups. They are necessary resources for school improvement; they are also necessary agents of change in a system that is increasingly distanced from those it serves.

We have chosen to center this discussion on the empowerment of parents, teachers, and communities, because these constituencies represent the most independent variables in the school change equation. While the entire range of school constituents deserves attention, many of the issues we raise can be applied to other school personnel, to specific community interests, and particularly to students, who at the secondary level should be considered significant participants in any school change process. Local school administrators are also distinct and important actors, who have received considerable attention in recent school research. We have focused on some basic issues concerning their management and leadership roles.

## EMPOWERING PARENTS

Involving parents in the school life of their children and in education as a public institution is not a new idea for school improvement. In principle at least, the elected school board and PTA or PA systems were constructed in recognition of parents' legitimate rights of consultation and their important support role in the education process. However, the parent role has been auxiliary and advisory, at best. Most typically, parent involvement is a token formality in both school governance and in the classroom. The parents' place is generally usurped by administrators, experts, and politicians, who may or may not speak in their name.

Nonetheless, the benefits of parent participation are manifold. A number of studies show that active parent involvement in schooling is a consistent correlate of improved school performance; this finding is underscored in a recent report by the National Commission on Secondary Schooling for Hispanics.[1] Parents have a tangible impact on the motivation of students and teachers and on their expectations for achievement. Among the useful forms of parental influence are tutoring, co-learning, class visitation, extra-curricular activity, and consultation in individualized learning programs. Parents are also essential as advocates and monitors, especially in underserved communities, where struggles for access and entitlements remain central to educational opportunity. Parent advocacy for the individual student can spur the development of appropriate pedagogy and curriculum, as well as appropriate program and classroom placements. Parent activism as an element of school accountability has influenced the level of categorical funding, services for special needs, the procurement of teaching supplies and aids, the development of school performance information, and the quality of professional appointments. Parent involvement also affects school climate: it has an impact on teaching style, respect for cultural diversity, school order, observance of student rights, and cooperative practice among school people.[2]

With the decline of civil rights activism in the 1970s, widespread parent activism in urban, minority communities became more sporadic. The legacy of earlier organizing and recent battles over school funding cuts have spurred a number of local efforts to improve distressed urban schools, but without the context of an overarching social movement. In the absence of broader social activism, the intrinsic barriers to participation are more sharply felt. School advocacy organizations have identified these general problems:[3]

1. The majority of parents face consuming pressures of economic survival and family maintenance. For the poor, these pressures on time, energy, and income can be overwhelming. The need for both parents to work, the extraordinary burden on women heads of household, even the expense of child care and travel to attend school meetings are real factors limiting parent inclinations to activism.

2. Parents are often intimidated by cultural distances between themselves and school professionals. School practices are justified by educators who claim an expertise that working class and poor parents cannot match. Professional elitism fosters the perception of parents as an intrusion rather than a resource. It is ironic that those whom the schools have most failed are considered the least qualified to speak on educational defects. The gap is reinforced when school personnel are not indigenous to the school community. In New York City, for example, 75% of public school students are minorities, but 75% of the administrative and teaching staffs are not.

3. Parents are often uncertain about who is responsible for school failure. Professional mystification frequently carries the implicit message that parents are to blame for their children's underachievement or alienated attitudes toward school. Parents may well reciprocate by holding teachers solely responsible for deficient school performance. An interlocking cycle of blame develops and, with it, a pervasive negativism that discourages interaction and cooperation.

4. Parents lack clarity about what would improve the schools, which may reflect confusion among professionals as well. The absence of programmatic approaches to school improvement tends to isolate single issues, such as discipline, and tends to focus concern on the most tangible items, such as building repair. Qualitative learning issues that involve multiple and interrelated factors seem difficult to address with concrete recommendations.

5. Parents are shut out of the school governance process. The existing participatory mechanisms do not provide genuine authority over key aspects of school management, such as budget and personnel, and are often controlled by professionals. Frequently, parent consultations are perfunctory and meetings are dominated by administrators. Beyond the local school, the bureaucratic structures of education, which have expanded considerably with the extension of mass public schooling, also pose formidable barriers. Education is one of the most complex of all social institutions—it has parallel governance and administrative hierarchies and multiple levels of authority, from the quasi-autonomous district to local, state, and federal agencies. The complexity of the apparatus is inhibiting enough, but there is also a politics behind it. The centers of decision-making are systematically distanced from the local school, the level at which parents can most readily organize and sustain influence. It should not be sur-

prising that parent disaffection is as often the expression of realism as of apathy.

## Breaking Down the Barriers

Overwhelming as these barriers to parent involvement appear, there are signs that parent activism is reviving, particularly in the elementary schools. Parent-teacher organizations report that membership is at its highest levels since the early 1970s; the number of parents working as volunteers in schools has doubled in ten years to around 5 million in 1980.[4] Observers have noted that this resurgence may represent a largely middle-class trend, corresponding to concern over a shrinking school revenue base and alarm triggered by the national commissions. Nonetheless, while barriers to participation remain high for working parents and single parents and for poor and undereducated parents, successful efforts to stimulate and support their activism suggest that avenues for more widescale participatory reform can be opened.

Fiscal crises and the deterioration of urban school systems have prompted the formation of several impressive public coalitions around the country, acting as political pressure groups and cultivating active parent constituencies. Such groups include the Philadelphia Parents Union for Public Schools, New York's Educational Priorities Panel, New Jersey's Institute for Citizen Involvement in Education, the Chicago Citizens Panel on School Finance, the Education Campaign of the Citizens Education Center Northwest (Seattle), and Parents United for Full Public School Funding in Washington, D.C.

Many of these groups have moved beyond fiscal issues to address school improvement needs, including parent involvement, curriculum development, and supportive services. The Philadelphia Parents Union has initiated a three-year parent workshop program, reaching 3,000 public school families, to ensure that new curricular, testing, and disciplinary standards are implemented to increase access, equity, and parent participation. The Education Campaign has conducted local public meetings across Washington State to build an agenda for comprehensive legislative reform of school finance, governance, and standards. Parents United has successfully restored staffing and budget cuts in the District of Columbia school system, and, in the process, they have developed parent membership in eighty local schools, affiliations with forty-seven local school administrations, and a foundation to sponsor locally initiated enrichment projects.

There is a wide range of concerns that stimulate parent organizing, apart from critical funding and instructional issues. A unique parent organizing campaign, the Asbestos in Schools Project, has developed in New Jersey to remove asbestos hazards from school buildings. In the process, parents have challenged school budget controls, designed state legislation, and sparked other parent groups to organize on the asbestos danger nationally. Low-income parents have responded to the weakening of earlier Title I guidelines for parent involvement, which included explicit requirements for parent participation, consultation, and training through Parent Advisory Councils (PACs). Spearheaded by the national Title I/Chapter 1 Parent Coalition and state affiliates, parent activists are looking to both Congress and the states to restore strong PAC mandates.

Perhaps the best overall example of sustained and effective parent involvement is found in Head Start, where many mandated parent councils have played highly activist roles in managing and operating centers, and where parents have been hired and trained to work as paraprofessionals in the program. Extending the council concept to regular schools, states such as California, South Carolina, and Florida have mandated parent participation in local school councils, with varying degrees of authority over budget and policy decisions. The Institute for Responsive Education (IRE) and the National Committee for Citizens in Education (NCCE) have developed models of local school governance in districts across the country. These programs provide clearly defined roles for parents, and work to implement participatory school-based management systems in low-income communities.

Effective Schools research has also been utilized to develop tools for parent investigation and monitoring of school performance. The Effective Schools movement, initiated by educators over the past decade, has systematically identified characteristics of successful schools in distressed school systems. Through both research and demonstration projects, the movement has established the types of positive school intervention that surmount educational disadvantages. Using several variants of Effective Schools criteria, more than a dozen state education departments have developed school assessment instruments for local school improvement programs. The NCCE, the Council for Basic Education (CBE), and the Center for Early Adolescence (CEA) have developed school evaluation guides for parents. Effective Schools research has also been used to design parent-training curricula by local advocacy and citizen action groups, including the Southeastern Public Education Program, Schoolwatch in New Jersey, Designs for Change in Chicago, and Advocates for Children in New York.

Apart from these organized initiatives, there are also spontaneous examples of school-sponsored programs, union-sponsored programs, and parent associations that have developed mechanisms for increasing parent participation. These mechanisms include raising funds to pay stipends to parent representatives, providing subsidies to meet travel and child-care expenses, running workshops on school administration and instruction, developing parent/child co-learning programs, and offering advocacy training.

Campaigns for school accountability, when they engage and inform parents in a genuine attempt at reform, show that barriers to participation can be transcended and that a sophisticated and resilient core of local school activists can be formed. Through sustained organizing, parents can overcome intimidation and self-blame, can offer constructive criticism and assistance, can focus on issues that are central to improvement, and can create participatory vehicles. The key, however, is generating a parallel institutional commitment to reform that recognizes the citizenship rights of parents in shaping school change. Such institutional commitment must include openness to structural reform in the policy-making and administrative process, so that parents become an established element of school authority. Parent involvement is most decisively discouraged when it does not make a difference. The incentives for parent participation do not arise out of moral or civic duties, but because children's well-being is at stake *and* because real possibilities exist to influence the outcome in an ongoing way.

Several structural approaches to promote parent empowerment have been raised or revived in the national school debate. One promising concept is the school-site council, or school-site management approach, already mentioned in passing; we will discuss this concept and related issues of local school governance in the next chapter. Here we address an idea that has become more widely fashionable in school policy circles, the concept of parent (and student) choice exercised through optional enrollment or voucher systems.

## Parent Choice and Voucher Systems

There is a growing call to restructure schools to compete for enrollments on the basis of performance and specialized programs. Fifteen states have recently developed initiatives in this area, some proposing tuition voucher systems. Given the vigor with which optional enrollment and voucher concepts are being espoused, it is important to clarify the different forms they take, as well as the dangers and potentials they represent in practice.

First, there can be no mistaking that the voucher programs advocated by the Right, including the Reagan administration's TEACH proposal cited earlier, are designed to promote public funding of private education and the eventual displacement of public education. This intent was explicitly expressed in a recent commentary in the Heritage Foundation's *Education Update*, which urged Christian educators to support the TEACH initiative. The article states: "Americans interested in educational reform need to pursue the dual strategy of deregulation and educational choice. The Chapter 1 voucher, if passed, surely will be the forerunner of a much more fundamental and comprehensive move to restructure the U.S. educational system through a general voucher. Therefore, steps must be taken to reduce the threat of regulation accompanying a voucher program."[5]

Clearly, the ultra-conservative version of vouchers is directed by the broader policy goal of divesting government services in favor of the private sector, including, in the case of education, religious institutions. At stake is not only the viability of public school services but, as these conservatives note, the public's capacity to regulate its investment in education. By eroding or dismantling coherent public school systems, by dispersing enrollments and atomizing parents into individual consumers, such voucher systems provide ample opportunity both to undermine community accountability and to circumvent mandates protecting both civil and equity rights. This danger is heightened by the Supreme Court's retreat on civil rights enforcement, from the *Bakke* decision to the *Grove City* decision. *Grove City* bans discriminatory practices only in the specific program or department that receives federal funds, regardless of the discriminatory practices of the institution as a whole. The Reagan administration goes further by claiming that vouchers, since given to parents, do not even qualify as federal funding to institutions.[6]

When vouchers are proposed entirely within the public education system, they present somewhat different potentials, although a parallel set of concerns. One immediate concern is that public voucher plans clear the path for extending vouchers into private schooling. This is certainly one motive behind conservative support for the choice movement in public schools. Yet if we set aside this political consideration, what are the positive and negative arguments for public school voucher plans?

Public school vouchers are intended to encourage wider educational options and allow parents and students to vote with their feet on the ability of individual schools to meet standards and expectations. In theory, this voucher concept endorses the expansion of alternative approaches and the flexibility of the system to meet the diverse needs it encompasses. Schools that do not suit a significant level of parent/student preferences or do not live up to their program goals would be faced with declining enrollments, not just declining test scores. Presumably, the result would be a mix of decent schools, from the traditional neighborhood school to the curriculum-specialized school to the pedagogically specialized school—and poorly functioning schools would simply go out of business.

But the theory of the open market is not the same as its practice. Where conditions throughout a school district are fairly equivalent, where populations are homogeneous and transportation feasible, it is possible that local schools will have equal resources to develop responsive programs and that students will have even chances of selecting an appropriate enrollment. Yet apart from some suburban school districts, most systems start with wide differentials between schools and between students. Enrollment options may compound these differentials by creaming the best-prepared students into limited, select institutions—leaving only undesirable and neglected schools for disadvantaged students to choose among. Choices in the school marketplace can end up as they do in the economic marketplace, where low-income consumers are free to live in tenements, free to pay higher prices in ghetto stores, free to compete for too few jobs, but not free or welcome to live somewhere else.

The New York City experience with specialized high schools, often called magnet schools, illustrates the double-edged potentials of optional enrollment systems. In New York, where magnet schools can draw enrollment across the city through competitive admissions, a four-tiered structure has emerged that puts the comprehensive neighborhood high school in serious jeopardy. The top-ranked academic high schools cream the most achieving and advantaged students out of the local school. A second level of specialized theme schools, and a third level of vocational high schools, cater to the middle range of students and also draw off teaching resources in a particular field. What is left at the bottom is the neighborhood high school, with a restricted basic curriculum, the highest concentration of disadvantaged and poorly prepared students, and the most hard-pressed teachers.

Many of New York's neighborhood high schools are little different today from the child warehouses faced by immigrants in the past, only now the students are overwhelmingly black and Latino. Counseling and preparation for high school selection and entry are grossly deficient in the intermediate schools, so that students without independent resources cannot exercise meaningful or informed choices. Similarly, parents with no prior understanding of the option system and minimal contact with teachers and counselors have little chance of guiding their children or intervening to assure the best placement. Moreover, students who do not make the grade in the schools of their choice are thrown back into inadequate and devalued neighborhood schools. Economic and racial segregation have not been dissipated, but reinforced.[7]

The New York example suggests that an optional enrollment system that does not equalize resources, mandate open admissions and retention, expand guidance services for parents and students, and simultaneously upgrade the quality of comprehensive schools can become another mechanism for stratification and segregation. There are instances, however, where carefully designed and contained option systems appear to meet these criteria and work well. One example, also from New York City, is the optional enrollment plan used in Community School District 4 among East Harlem's elementary schools. Another example is the Medford District magnet program in Massachusetts, which was initiated in 1970 as the result of a desegregation order. Medford's

Hervey school succeeded as a multi-racial magnet by offering many special features: single sessions, smaller classes, a multi-cultural education program, media and computer centers, an all-day kindergarten, door-to-door busing, and strong parent participation. Even with cutbacks and the closing of Hervey, the experiment has continued through the Brooks-Hobbs School. One critical condition of the Medford success was that it operated within one district, in a population where racial balance was not difficult to achieve.[8]

Geographic scope is an essential consideration in optional enrollment or voucher systems. For the danger that voucherized schooling will be less accessible and responsive to parents and communities exists in public school option designs as well as in those that apply to private education. Parent choices about the education of their children should not begin and end with the selection of the school; and community accountability is not satisfied solely by parent choice. Some public voucher proposals advocate that competitive enrollment systems be established over wide areas, even statewide, as is now the case in Minnesota.[9] In such dispersed systems, disadvantaged children and parents will typically be the ones to travel and bear the costs of choice. Disadvantaged communities, particularly inner cities and rural townships, may well lose their local school institutions. Working parents, taxpayers, and citizens will be further removed from the practical conduct of the school, concentrating greater control in the hands of school professionals and state administrators. Some schools may gain from a community of purpose, but there is also a community of people, a social and civic life, that schools should be rooted within and draw upon. We do not need to make schools worlds unto themselves to make them better; we need, in fact, to open schooling to the world that is shaping children and families.

Clearly, diverse school environments can benefit students, as demonstrated by the success of many alternative schools, and alternative programs within schools, over the past decade. Clearly, voluntary options in school and program assignments, for teachers as well as parents and students, can increase motivation and engagement. Clearly, the reconstruction of enrollment patterns across heterogeneous socioeconomic and racial groups can promote equity and opportunity. Yet public voucher systems and magnet schools are not, in themselves, sufficient strategies for meeting these goals or for fostering school improvement. Where optional enrollment systems function as open markets with scarce resources, elitist sorting processes will prevail; students will not participate equally in selecting schools and schools will not function equitably in selecting students. However, where enrollment options are part of a larger commitment to enrich disadvantaged schools, to accommodate all varieties of need, and to stimulate community access, they may well enhance innovation, involvement, and meaningful choice.

Voucher concepts confined to public schooling can thus be vehicles for either divestiture or diversity, and the politics of schooling, not the abstract merits of choice, will determine which. In today's context, where meritocratic concepts prevail and educational stratification is accelerating, public school vouchers must be closely scrutinized for their impacts on equity, civic accountability, and community integrity. Moreover, the present politics of schooling mean that we cannot disregard the privatization agenda of the right-wing choice movement and its vision of the educational marketplace. The fact that vouchers, public or private, have become their opening wedge for the deregulation and atomization of public commitments to education must weigh heavily in the debate. If we have learned anything from twenty years of school reform, it is that influence over the implementation of social policy counts far more than good intentions.

## EMPOWERING TEACHERS

The debate over the role of teachers in school decision-making has polarized around issues of autonomy and accountability. Highly bureaucratic administrative structures often strip teachers of the opportunity to shape their work creatively. Excessive standardization—along with large classes, supervisory duties, excessive paperwork, and fragmented work periods—reduce teachers to caretakers and technicians. Limited in-service training, inadequate continuing education, low pay, and low status contribute to teachers' sense of isolation and demoralization. Teachers themselves, in responding to these pressures, may also mistrust innovation, compound the rigidities of the system, and assume adversarial positions toward community demands. At times, this siege mentality has overcome teacher associations as well. Hence, we often encounter what seems a deadlocked contradiction between oppressive authority and passive resistance. But the contradiction flows from a single source: school institutions that do not respect teachers' professional integrity and do not allow frontline staff to share decision-making power.

To understand the ambiguous ways teachers are situated in the schools, we need first to look at the processes that have devalued education as a vocation and a social service. This devaluation has involved a curious interweaving of trends emanating from the expansion of mass education in the post-war period. The baby boom, rising occupational and income standards, and popular demands for broader access brought an influx of teachers into a rapidly centralizing system. The teaching workforce was transformed from what had been in large part an educated woman's calling to a more diverse body of service professionals working as public employees within an enlarged and increasingly hierarchic institution. The pervasive outcome, both for teachers and for local school communities, has been to raise new barriers and distances in decision-making at both instructional and institutional levels.

As post-war public education consolidated, teachers experienced increased need and opportunity for professional organization. By the mid-1960s, teacher organizing coincided with and reflected the upsurge in social activism among minorities, students, and public employees across the society. However, the channeling of teacher organizing into craft union formations in many cases produced a divergence from and conflict with its social movement context. There was a particularly sharp estrangement between the American Federation of Teachers and the urban civil rights movement, which initiated community drives for school accountability and control over new school resources. In the notorious case of New York City, where minorities struggled for decentralization in the late '60s, the bureaucratic and political apparatus was able to enlist the union as an ally against community activism. In return for extended collective bargaining rights and higher pay, the union tended to narrow its concept of self-interest along traditional craft or guild lines: raising technical barriers to accreditation, enhancing its bargaining power as a special and exclusive constituency, defending job rights through its lobbying clout and through legalistic regulations.

Of course, there is real variety in how teachers' unions

function locally, reflecting the size of the given school system, its governance mechanisms, state labor laws, the collective bargaining history, and rank-and-file attitudes. In addition, there are a number of significant philosophical differences at the national level between the American Federation of Teachers (AFT) and the National Education Association (NEA).

The national AFT has a tradition of bargaining militance, reflecting the concentration of its 610,000 members in the older urban school systems. But the AFT has often been criticized for its resistance to social justice issues, its special interest politics, and its autocratic leadership style. The national NEA represents 1.7 million teachers in suburban, rural, and newer urban districts. It has a consistently progressive record on social justice issues and also an impressive degree of formal democracy. Yet NEA has been faulted for being overly defensive in education policy, and for relying on its size to exercise professional leverage, rather than developing potentially broad links to public constituencies.

Apart from these differences, teacher organizations in general face the problem that bureaucratic unionism has become a prevalent response to bureaucratic employer control, a substitute for the power teachers need over their immediate work environment. At the state and local levels, there is a tendency to reduce the collective support teachers need on the job to a reliance on the union apparatus at the bargaining table or legislative committee room. There is a tendency to reduce struggle over working conditions to brokering over terms of employment. A classic example is the AFT's pursuit of higher compensation, while for many years avoiding the issue of lowering class size—a position akin to demanding combat pay without questioning why the troops are at war.

Today's new pressure for teacher accountability—in the form of technical performance criteria, competency testing, and the standardization of curriculum and pedagogy—place new demands on the unions to broaden their roles in the school change debate. Thus far, both the NEA and AFT have mixed records in responding to the challenge.

The NEA has been outspoken in resisting elitist concepts of reform, in regard to students as well as teachers. It has strongly defended entitlement programs, combatted the "choice" movement, and disputed quantitative approaches to raising standards. It has been highly visible in opposing merit pay and teacher testing as arbitrary and insulting performance measures. It has also used its political clout at the state level to counter mounting rightwing attacks on teacher integrity and academic freedom, attacks that frequently spearhead more general assaults on public education. On the other hand, the NEA has not developed an energetic proactive campaign that raises programmatic alternatives on issues such as teacher improvement and the restructuring of school governance. By sticking to reactive postures, the NEA too often ends up defending the profession and the school institution as they are.

The AFT's role in the debate is almost the mirror image of the NEA's. The AFT has focused on issues of professional upgrading and teacher autonomy, voicing strong support for teacher involvement in school decision-making, more flexible approaches to classroom management, and alternative accountability systems such as peer evaluation. At the same time, the AFT has not challenged the meritocratic framework of the excellence movement on issues of student performance and achievement. The AFT has not been a prominent voice on equity issues and the crisis of inner-city schools, beyond its predictable opposition to cutbacks in education funding and to private school voucher plans. By centering its concern on the status of the profession—while ignoring the impacts that more competitive and punitive standards will have on underserved students—the AFT has not adequately addressed a fundamental condition of teaching, the status of children in stratified school systems.

For all of their limitations, however, teachers' unions are more than a fact of life in education; they are a legitimate and necessary vehicle for protecting job rights. School boards and administrators are no more enlightened employers than steel corporations, and the union is often a scapegoat for mismanagement and employer intransigence. The courts are distinctly hostile to public employees, and educators have no immunity to economic contraction or political backlash. The problem is that many teachers' unions have become trapped at an early point of development in defensive and exclusive postures, in parochial professionalism. On issues of democratic education, including teacher autonomy and institutional responsiveness, the unions have too often balked.

## Beyond Craft Unionism

If teachers are to develop as a school constituency, and not simply as a special interest, efforts are needed to recast the craft union role and to renew the tradition of social unionism. One improvement lies in the broader exercise of local union democracy, where teachers reclaim their own organizations as vehicles for influencing teaching conditions. A second advance lies in connecting union locals with community constituents in developing common programs for school improvement. An encouraging move in both these directions was taken in 1983 by the Massachusetts Teachers Association in its *Education for Democracy Program,* a long-term plan for involving the union in progressive school reform, strengthening its locals and membership participation, and initiating better ties with community organizations.[10] A third step forward lies in extending union involvement in educational needs beyond support for positive legislation. A recent example is the NEA's Operation Rescue, a $2 million fund created at the 1984 national assembly to aid local drop-out prevention programs.

A fourth area of critical importance is for the unions to embrace affirmative action in the teaching profession. Given recent Supreme Court decisions, the commitment to affirmative action will require new approaches, with an emphasis on recruitment, on hiring and assignment practices, and on career development opportunities. The economic and social climate of the '80s is already taking its toll, reducing the college entry of minorities and their representation in tomorrow's professional pool. In 1977, 50% of all black high school graduates enrolled in college, but by 1982, the figure had fallen to 36%. The percentage of white high school graduates enrolling in college remained steady at just over 50%.[11] Teachers' unions can be a significant political voice for reversing these trends, particularly by insisting on affirmative action goals in programs to meet the looming teacher shortage. The commitment to racial equality in education goes hand in hand with a vision of social unionism among teachers. Such a commitment serves a profession that needs new members, and serves schools that need more appropriate racial and cultural balance in staffing.

Improving professional development services is another priority for teacher activism, and an opportunity for unions to play supportive roles. The poverty of current in-service training and staff development programs is particularly acute and appears repeatedly in studies of teacher needs. The teacher center concept has emerged in recent years as a national movement addressing this problem. The centers promote teacher-directed in-service training by providing time and space for peer discussion, the exploration of new materials and techniques, the evaluation of school and classroom problems. Teacher centers have been established in a variety of local forms. They function within or across individual schools, within or across district lines, and also by grade and subject groupings. They have been sponsored by school districts, by independent groups of teachers, and by local unions. One promising example is the Special Educator Support Program, sponsored by the United Federation of Teachers in New York City. The program provides peer assistance to teachers working in special education classrooms, which are chronically underfunded and often staffed on an emergency basis.

The North Dakota Study Group provides another model for teacher development initiatives. The group works through correspondence, publications, workshops, and conferences to disseminate open classroom theory to a wide network of members across the country. It focuses on linking an understanding of child development with pedagogical theory and practice. It stresses methods of peer evaluation and joint teacher/parent assessment systems. The North Dakota Study Group has been instrumental in developing concepts of teacher autonomy that emphasize the centrality of teachers in the school community and the need for supportive approaches to accountability.[12]

A final element of professional revaluation is the need for teachers to participate in school management and governance. It is ironic that education conservatives of all stripes are calling for the restoration of teacher authority over students, but ignore the issue of teacher authority in the institution. Power-sharing is essential to creating an environment of collective support and to valuing the skills and effort of the profession. Teachers' unions have shown increasing interest in participatory school governance approaches, but it is important to understand that this is not a process that can be effectively mediated by the union alone. Professional authority should not be reduced to a single classroom, the bargaining table, or the school board meeting, although it should be felt in those places.

Professional authority needs to be exercised collaboratively by all staff members on all issues that shape the organization of the local school in an ongoing way. Teachers need to be recognized as key actors in a decision-making process that offers substantive control over the uses of testing, the selection of curricula, the construction of pedagogy, the linkage to supportive services, student grouping and placement, hiring and promotional ladders, the use of time and space, the purchase of supplies, and the fiscal priorities of the school program. Almost every in-depth study of current school practice concludes that a central determinant of good schooling is good teachers. Yet we must be clear that what makes most teachers good is not a mystical talent for rising above adversity, but the opportunity to shape the conditions and consequences of their work.

Recognition of the need for teacher empowerment has been growing in the current school debate. At the same time, the volume of prescriptive legislation and quick-fix formulas is rapidly multiplying. Even in the best programs for school reform, this tension between bottom-up and top-down approaches surfaces repeatedly. Perhaps the most interesting case is the Effective Schools movement, whose research powerfully confirms the value of a school-centered change process that engages teachers. Yet among the various programs utilizing Effective Schools research, there is a growing split between those that stress the importance of teacher-directed change within participatory school cultures and those that magnify the leadership function of administrators and policy officials.

## The Effective Schools Movement

The Effective Schools movement has made several breakthroughs in school reform research and thinking. The foremost contribution, initiated by Ron Edmunds, is in demonstrating that poor school performance is not inevitable for children who are economically or socially deprived, but is a function of specific school practice. Put another way, the Effective Schools movement has identified schools that are instructionally effective in the most disadvantaged circumstances, showing that students' social backgrounds do not set limits on school achievement. The implications are profound in terms of prevailing myths about performance. By finding that school practice determines low or high achievement, either reproducing disadvantage or surmounting it, we dispel the notion that schools do not make a difference and the idea that schools cannot shoulder responsibility for equality of results. Further, by identifying the school characteristics associated with improving performance, Effective Schools research helps explain why successful schools are not more common and what approaches can raise the chances of success.

Another set of breakthroughs has been made by the Effective Schools' focus on the local school culture and on multi-dimensional approaches to change. The research has shown that there are no single or static ingredients that produce effective schooling, but rather multiple, interrelated factors that add up to supportive or disabling conditions in the learning process. Effective Schools research has not established precise causal factors, and more extensive and sophisticated study needs to be done, but it has defined correlates of good schooling. The seven correlates now most familiar in the literature are: clear school mission, high expectations for all students, strong instructional leadership, opportunity to learn (time on task), a stable and orderly school climate, frequent monitoring of pupil achievement, and close school/home relations.

The Effective Schools movement has been highly influential in generating practice from its research, laying the basis for new school improvement projects across the country. It is now estimated that at least eight states have incorporated Effective Schools findings into their school improvement policies, and several others have adopted aspects of the research. In 1983, Effective Schools projects were located in twenty-five states, covering 875 school districts.[13] As Effective Schools concepts have been applied in school improvement projects, the debate over the interpretation of the effectiveness criteria has grown, particularly over the reliance on standardized testing as the measure of performance. The criteria themselves have been refined, and more varied sets of criteria have emerged, reflecting different tendencies within the Effective Schools movement.

The divergence in Effective Schools approaches has developed over the "process" issues involved in instituting Effective Schools designs. The movement is not immune to the one-best-system syndrome. Side by side with many exciting school improvement initiatives are some disturbing trends.

The stress on instructional leadership, for instance, has been used to create a "super-principal" concept, where change hinges solely on the dynamism and authority of the principal. No one disputes the advantages of having administrators who are dynamic leaders, and the difficulty of improving schools where principals are deficient. But a good principal does not single-handedly transform a troubled school. The great leader theory of school change too easily becomes a cop-out, a way to ignore the interaction of the entire school community, a way to fix blame for failure or monopolize credit for success. The super-principal concept is also a distortion of Effective Schools research, which has found varied sources of instructional leadership in improving schools, especially high schools.

Another problematic direction involves the attempt to construct mechanistic templates for school improvement, designed by academic researchers and imposed by school bureaucracies from the top down. In this approach, the focus has been on raising test scores, rationalizing management controls, standardizing teaching styles, and regulating planning procedures—replete with timetables and checklists—that are presumed to guarantee that effective measures will be instituted. Although mandates can stimulate genuine reform processes at the local level, the top-down approach to implementation defeats the spirit of initiative and collaboration essential to motivating teachers and improving school cultures.

Moreover, top-down mandates have a tendency to change schools' reporting styles more than the substance of their practice. As states and districts routinize Effective Schools programs, we can unhappily imagine a new scramble to be designated an instructionally effective school on the basis of adept public relations or central office favoritism. We conclude that where Effective Schools concepts are reduced to technocratic formulas and management control systems, the likely results will be both a failure to achieve meaningful school improvement and the discrediting of reform impulses. In this case, Effective Schools concepts will become another passing fashion, among so many in education.[14]

These cautions should not detract, however, from the encouraging developments occurring within the Effective Schools Movement. With the practical experience of school improvement projects, greater stress has been placed on the importance of a collaborative, internally motivated school change process.[15] There is new emphasis on fostering local initiatives and developing local strategies, using the research as a guidepost, not a template. Successful projects tend to involve all staff in developing evaluation criteria over a wide range of practices. They promote teacher initiative in planning organizational as well as instructional reforms. A growing number of successful projects also promote principles of participatory governance and cultivate parent activism. The Effective Schools movement has begun to redefine its essential criteria to include these process issues. The criteria synthesized by Purkey and Smith are among the most comprehensive, and incorporate the study of organization theory, systems innovation theory, and workplace reform. They offer thirteen factors that interactively contribute to positive school culture and improved school performance:[16]

1. School-site management and democratic decision-making.
2. Strong leadership from administrators, teachers, or teams of both.
3. Staff stability.
4. A planned, coordinated curriculum with in-depth study.
5. Schoolwide staff development.

6. Parental involvement and support.
7. Schoolwide recognition of academic success.
8. Maximized active learning time in academic areas.
9. District support for local school efforts.
10. Collaborative planning and collegial relationships.
11. Sense of community.
12. Clear goals and high expectations commonly shared.
13. Order and discipline established through consensus.

The Purkey and Smith criteria focus on teachers, which seems justified in terms of the pivotal role they must play in each of the assessment, planning, implementing, and evaluating phases of a school improvement project. These criteria confirm the central importance of the teacher empowerment issue in how we judge school reform proposals. At the same time, teachers are only one key part of the school decision-making process. As we noted in the previous section, Effective Schools criteria have been quite successfully used by parents in initiating school improvement projects. The general lesson seems to be that where the Effective Schools approach is adapted to specific local conditions—and where it is used not only as a procedure for assessment but also as a process for empowering the entire school community—it offers real potential for generating progressive reforms that are thorough and sustained. Again, the constituency politics of schools will be crucial in determining whether the strengths of Effective Schools concepts are further developed or debased.

## EMPOWERING COMMUNITIES

Although schools are essentially local institutions, they are frequently isolated from the communities they serve. The distance of schools from communities is in part the product of the bureaucratization of educational policy we have cited in regard to the erosion of parental and teacher authority. This distance also stems from a more general concentration of power in the hands of political elites. Moreover, the prevailing notion that schools should be worlds unto themselves, with a distinction between academic and social missions, reinforces the alienation of schools from their community context.

In asserting that the isolation of schools from communities undermines school performance, we need first to clarify what is meant by community. The term should signify much more than local civic leadership, those citizens most widely referred to in appeals for citizen support of education. Local elites often do come to stand for "the community" when grassroots forces are not active, but elites do not necessarily share the same interests or options as parents, alumni, taxpayers, voters, workers, homemakers, retirees, church members, shopkeepers, social service providers—the entire range of citizens who, in multiple roles, comprise the community for which education is a vital function and institution.

Yet when we equate community with the grassroots citizenry, it is not always easy to set parameters. In many places across America, schools serve self-contained residential areas and relatively homogeneous or integrated population groups. But in other places, especially urban areas, school districts encompass widely divergent residential areas and groups of people. Here the sense of community is often defined by ethnic, socio-economic, and political status, which may or may not coincide with housing and school enrollment patterns. In some suburban areas, populations are not necessarily stable and there may be little sense of community at all.

When we talk of the relationship of schools to communities, we obviously must consider the specific realities. Some schools will face the problem that the community defined by service from a local school or school district will not be coherent in other respects, including its expectations for education. Some schools will find that their service community is deeply divided on priorities and goals for school performance. Some schools may even find significant sectors of the community antagonistic to public education or resentful of the resources devoted to it. Nor are local communities, even those with a strong consensus, the sole or sacred arbitor of educational needs. Other democratic principles—including human rights, civil liberties, civic pluralism, and the needs of youth—are essential to the public interest in education.

Nonetheless, we cannot construct a democratic mission for public schooling without taking on the task of involving local communities, however they present themselves, in the educational process. School isolation works to deny students a link between what they learn in the classroom and the environment they function in outside the school. The lack of relevance and connection is particularly acute for minority and low-income students, whose social and cultural background is not reflected, or is negatively reflected, in standard curricula based on a white, middle-class mainstream and on elitist structures of achievement. Isolation also denies communities the potentially integrative and empowering capacities of the school as a community institution. School isolation denies citizens an arena where differences can be recognized and common interests forged.

Finally, isolation denies schools the energy, the resources, and, ultimately, the allegiance of community members.

The consequences of this isolation are becoming especially damaging in the face of the growing and changing social problems we cited earlier: chronic unemployment, decaying social and physical infrastructures, shifting family and childraising patterns, and rising personal distress. These conditions are found in a wide range of rural, urban, and industrial communities and have enormous impact on how children function in school. Yet, in too many places, the school retreats further into its fortress mentality, resenting additional demands and seeking new ways to exclude disadvantaged youth or deny responsibility for their needs. Whether beleaguered or indifferent, school authorities have not generally embraced the task of initiating stronger linkages with other human services agencies, with community organizations, and with the youth, parents, local school employees, and neighborhood leaders who represent natural school constituencies. And, as we will discuss in the following chapter, school governance mechanisms rarely represent a genuine grassroots base.

Even apart from the political reforms that are needed to reassert community control in schooling, school authorities and staff can build constructive relationships with local forces. Schools can also find new ways to integrate themselves in communities as local public institutions. In the following discussion, we review two useful avenues for school outreach using advocacy organizations and local paraprofessionals. We then turn to ways that schools can serve and be served by community resources, including the open facility, school-based social services, economic and community development linkages, community literacy campaigns, and youth service work.

## School and Community Linkages

Youth advocacy organizations can be particularly useful in mediating school and community relations. Many advocacy groups have long-standing, if sometimes adversarial, involvement in education issues. The National Coalition of Advocates for Students, for instance, has nineteen affiliated organizations, operating in fifteen major cities and a number of rural regions, and includes national legal centers. Advocacy organizations not only represent parents and students in administrative hearings and appeals, but often organize and train parents and community groups in how to secure children's schooling rights and how to utilize the available channels of participation and redress effectively. Advocacy centers have accumulated valuable information on school performance, on patterns of access, discipline, and misclassification abuse, on corrective action and successful alternative programs. That experience could be well utilized in school planning and assessment, particularly in prevention and early intervention programs around issues such as school order and drop-outs. Advocacy groups are usually professionally run organizations that cannot, or should not, substitute for the voices of community members. But those advocacy groups that give priority to organizing as well as providing service at the grassroots level can be a valuable conduit for community concerns.

Another readily available resource for building school/community links and improving school climate is using local residents as paraprofessionals. In more privileged school systems, volunteers often serve as tutors, teacher aides, and special instructors. For working class and poor communities, however, it is necessary to provide paid jobs. By 1982, there were an estimated 150,000 paid paraprofessionals in education. The examples of Head Start and the Career Opportunities Program (COP, 1970–77), and the increasing use of paraprofessionals in special education, demonstrate a wide range of benefits. Community members working as paraprofessionals help to develop culturally appropriate curricula and teaching styles, bringing into the school a body of skills and social knowledge that remains outside most teacher-training experiences. They offer students a connection to the world beyond the school; not coincidentally, they have been effective in programs to establish more orderly schools and in a guidance capacity in drop-out programs. Paraprofessionals allow greater flexibility in the use of teacher time and are a key element in reducing teacher/student ratios, reducing teacher isolation in the classroom, encouraging small instructional groupings, and diffusing the non-instructional workload.[17]

In addition, the use of local paraprofessionals is a concrete mechanism for increasing school accountability to the community. If parents are to become an effective school constituency, paraprofessionals can serve as informed representatives, an activating and a mediating group. While not immune to pressure as school employees, they do not stand apart from the community and their relationships to family, neighbors, and local institutions. Paraprofessional employment has also been a route into the teaching profession, particularly when accompanied by opportunities for in-service and academic training. Where paraprofessionals are simply added on to traditional school practices, usually in non-instructional and clerical roles, their impact will be marginal. Where paraprofessionals are used as a restructuring resource—to enhance collaboration and flexibility in instruction and management, and to maximize community outreach—they can be a significant instrument of school change.

## The School as a Community Institution

School efforts to tap community resources and develop supportive constituencies can be strengthened by efforts to use school resources for the community. Improving school services, generating citizen interest and participation, and enriching the social fabric children grow up in are mutually reinforcing activities. The neighborhood school is ideally suited to serve as a community institution that reaches beyond the immediate school population and beyond academic functions. In low-income communities, where both schools and other social services are pervasively deficient, the need to enlarge and maximize the use of school resources is pressing. We see three areas that cultivate community school institutions: the open facility, school-based youth services, and school linkages with community development activity.

There are models, particularly those developed at the height of community activism in the late '60s, of the school that is open from early morning to evening as a neighborhood center, with breakfast programs, pre-school and after-school recreation programs, adult education classes, childcare centers, and adult/child co-learning programs in subjects from computers to nutrition. Schools are equipped to serve as meeting sites, local athletic sponsors, and cultural centers for exhibits and performing arts. Where these activities now exist as an integral part of the school function, the sense of community access and of collective accountability is greatly enriched. Obstacles to opening up school facilities, such as increased custodial workloads, have been met by community

members' contributing to the maintenance of the school.
the school.

The school is also a highly appropriate site for the delivery
of youth service programs, whether offered by public agencies or by community-based organizations. Examples of successful in-school projects cover a wide range of services:
health education and assessment, substance abuse treatment, return-to-school support programs, childcare and family counseling for teen parents, work experience and job
placement, neighborhood tutoring, youth hotlines, runaway
counseling, and nutrition programs. School-based human
service delivery could go further by locating full-scale agency
branches, such as family service offices and health clinics,
within the school facility. The coordination of such programs not only increases their effectiveness, but also works
to transform the atmosphere, attitudes, and responsiveness
of schools as institutions. Broadening the neighborhood
school's concern for student academic performance to comprehensive concern for the entire range of youth survival and
growth would significantly reduce the distance between
school and community. Broadening the social resources
available within the school would also reduce the burden on
teachers to cope with problems they feel powerless to alter.[18]

Educational activity can also be successfully linked to
community development activity, improving both social and
economic infrastructures. Again the outstanding model is
the Head Start program. While Head Start centers vary in
performance, the agency's overall record demonstrates its
widespread and enduring benefits to early childhood learning. This success is closely related to Head Start's role in developing community resources. Head Start has been likened
to the creation of small business enterprises throughout
poor areas; in 1980, it employed 70,000 people in 2,000 com-

munities. A large number of these employees are local residents working as paraprofessionals. The program has also been economically beneficial to single parents who were able to take jobs because they could count on childcare. In addition, Head Start has played a crucial intermediary role in linking families to health, welfare, and other social services, and in utilizing those services within the program.

In many cases, Head Start has accorded a strong role to parents, both through the mandated advisory councils and through volunteer work, at times supported by stipends, training sessions, transportation, and social activities. Head Start also interacts with regular school institutions. Studies indicate that Head Start programs have drawn heavily on school personnel to provide technical assistance and to coordinate learning approaches: 87% of Head Start staff were in contact with teachers and 81% with school program coordinators. While only 10% of Head Start centers were operated by school systems, nearly 60% used school buildings. The impact on schools also included a measurable increase in parent activism as Head Start children entered the regular system. This "trickle-up" effect is also expressed by the number of current community leaders who were first activated by their involvement in Head Start. Head Start has provided unique leadership training experiences, producing a generation of activists in the inner cities and rural South.[19]

The Head Start experience is suggestive in several respects. It points to innovative ways that community development can be school-based and linked to school improvement. For instance, the reduction of class size could make a decisive difference in struggling urban schools, as a requisite for improving classroom conditions and as a catalyst for restructuring overall school practice. A campaign to reduce class size could well utilize the Head Start model for developing staff resources, employing community residents, involving parents in school management, generating an activist base for school funding, and providing a new source of community leadership.

At the same time, the Head Start experience also suggests that educational activity does not have to be school-based in order to have substantial impacts on students—and on schools themselves. We find two proposals for community-based education to be especially compelling: the public literacy campaign and the youth service corps. In our view, both concepts respond to the crisis of inequality in education and both can help shape the schools as more open and effective institutions.

## The Community-Based Literacy Campaign

The concept of a public literacy campaign, delivered through community service organizations, has attracted growing interest. The seeds of the idea already exist in "right to read" programs in Chicago and Philadelphia, sponsored by municipal governments and civic groups, and in roughly 6,000 literacy programs operated nationwide. Of these, 185 have been identified as independent, community-based programs and their record indicates widespread success.[20] However, the principal models for community-based literacy programs are in Third World countries, where populations have had little formal schooling and where the education sector is highly undeveloped. In this country, the structural underpinnings would be quite different.

A public literacy campaign would be directed at children in school and at out-of-school youth and adults who have considerable exposure to formal schooling but whose school experience has been largely negative. The key target group would be minority youth, who suffer 60–80% drop-out rates in urban high schools, both those who are out of school and those who are floundering. A successful campaign would be directed not only at basic skills but at reversing attitudes of self-blame, alienation, and lack of confidence that result from school failure.

Ideally, the campaign would offer communities a range of options in establishing localized literacy services. A program could operate walk-in community centers offering free literacy services and open enrollment. A program could also utilize community institutions such as churches, neighborhood associations, self-help groups, and community development agencies for recruitment and program delivery. A community literacy service corps could be organized to staff the centers, engaging teaching professionals, college and high school students, and literate community members, on both a paid and a volunteer basis. Independent community boards, similar to the Community Action Program (CAP) boards of the '60s, could be created to administer the programs. Or a community could designate an existing social service agency or consortium in which it had confidence to establish an administrative structure, using referenda or public hearing processes. Clearly, we are envisioning a campaign whose priority is mobilization—the mobilization of grassroots energies to tackle illiteracy as a collective social problem.

The usual welfare delivery models are not appealing. Welfare programs rely on professional service vendors, are administered by removed bureaucracies, herd the "clients" into segregated facilities, and reduce the public's sense of social responsibility to begrudgingly paying taxes. In-school models for remedial services are also limiting. School settings are not well suited to adults who already have poor associations with school environments. Generally, traditional classroom structures and instructional methods are used, if only because they are considered cost-effective. Yet traditional classrooms only work well with students who have already acquired the fundamentals of reading or who already read. A campaign to eradicate illiteracy requires more varied, innovative, and personalized approaches, without the stigmas of school failure.

Our concept of a literacy campaign views the right to read as a fundamental right in a democratic society. Again, while literacy is critical to economic survival, it is also an essential condition of personal and social empowerment. A community-based literacy program could well be integrated with other community activities that enhance this sense of empowerment. Literacy campaigns could be used as components in public or private employment projects that provide job training and community economic development. They can be the cornerstone of voter registration drives and citizenship programs. They can be linked to family services, tenant-managed housing programs, preventive health services, care for the elderly or young children.

The optimal campaign would be national in scope, sponsored by the federal government with direct grants to community boards or agencies. The scenario could be played out on a smaller scale, sponsored by states, counties, or municipalities. There is no question that a literacy campaign as we have conceived it involves a novel and certainly complex organizing effort, whatever its scale. Perhaps the closest American precedent is the massive literacy drive conducted among GIs in World War II or the southern voter registration drives of the early '60s. In our view, the effort would be rewarded not only by inroads against illiteracy but by new expectations for literacy and by broadly based activism around educational needs, which can then translate into new demands, models, and initiatives for improving local schools.

## Youth Community Service Corps

Schools have relied almost exclusively on career motivation to link students to the adult world. The result has always been contingent on what the job market really offers young people; as we have noted, today it offers limited opportunities for working class youth and truly dismal prospects for poor and minority youth. Given the economic outlook, the renewed emphasis on business partnerships and private sector job structures seems particularly overrated. Educators are often drawn to the concept as a way to cultivate private sector support for public education needs, but, as a service strategy, such partnerships necessarily work more as creaming mechanisms than as job creation mechanisms.

An alternative approach that has gained congressional attention, and earned an Executive Office veto, is the development of a national youth service corps. The classic model is the New Deal's Civilian Conservation Corps (CCC), along with the Works Progress Administration (WPA); successor programs from the '60s and '70s also offer rich experience, including the Youth Employment Demonstration Projects (YEDPA), under CETA, and the California Conservation Corps. Today, we have no federal commitment to public job creation, but there are a number of concrete proposals to revive the youth service model already in circulation. These include the bill to create an American Conservation Corps, which passed Congress in 1984 and was rejected by Reagan as representing a "discredited" approach to youth unemployment (the president prefers the sub-minimum wage).[21] A comprehensive proposal has been developed by the Roosevelt Centennial Youth Project in support of its concept of a Community Service Corps for sixteen- to twenty-one-year-olds, combined with a Stay-in-School program for fourteen- to twenty-one-year-olds.[22]

Broadly conceived, the youth service corps approach suggests multiple benefits. It could integrate educational services with job experience in a broad range of public sector economic development activity, from environmental services, to infrastructure reconstruction, to human services (including literacy). This approach seems especially warranted in poor communities where public resources are most critical in stemming the destruction of neighborhoods. Ideally, the program would offer open entry to youth of all educational and economic backgrounds, but be specially geared to meeting the needs of low-income youth and school drop-outs.

We also favor the creation of community service components within the standard high school curriculum. Again, the opportunities for local youth service placements are broad, from public housing renovation to social services, from cultural centers to subsidized community enterprises. School integration in these projects can involve youth in on-the-job training, enhancing career exploration, workplace exposure, and vocational skills. Schools can also incorporate community activity into social studies curricula, using restoration and service projects as field laboratories for student investigation and the enhancement of citizenship skills. The benefits to school and community are mutual and, most importantly, the linkage provides youth with ways to contribute directly to the improvement of their neighborhoods and their own futures in them.

## EMPOWERMENT IN EDUCATION

In relating school practice and school change to the role of parents, teachers, and communities, the central theme has been empowerment: the opportunity and means to effectively participate and share authority. Schools are not worlds unto themselves, which is why no one best school system can be devised, however many times the attempt has been made. If the mission of schooling is defined by democratic standards, schools must respond to the societal conditions that influence them in order to perform well for all students. To argue for the empowerment of school constituents is to recognize that they are essential elements of the school culture.

And if, as we contend, progressive reform in education does not fundamentally hinge on issues of technique, but rests on political choices and priorities, we must change the institutional politics of schooling. To argue for the empowerment of school constituents is thus also to recognize that they are indispensable agents of school improvement. Our goal is to add new forces to the institutional politics of schooling, to make school politics more participatory and more directed by the needs of the entire school community. To complete our argument, we turn now to the issues of authority and finance in education, the bottom-line issues of political power.

# 6.

# Governance and Funding: Toward Progressive Federalism

Historically, major involvement by parents, teachers, and community members has developed through self-organized movements of these constituents to alter school conditions, not as the result of policy mandates. Today, around the country, local education activists are deeply involved in grassroots school improvement campaigns. Yet too often their work remains peripheral, distanced by school authorities who prefer to contain citizen involvement within institutional partnerships. Too often activism remains defensive, a consuming battle to stop abuses or enforce entitlements, which continually pre-empts long-term designs for change. And, too often, the reforms achieved are hollow, thwarted by hostile institutions that outlast citizen action or simply denied the resources to take root.

These common experiences tell us that democratic politics require more than a clear and positive vision of change and more than grassroots participation. Both issues and activism are hard to sustain without achieving new structural mechanisms that allow popular control over resources and priorities—or at least allow an open contest for control to be waged in an ongoing way. An objective, then, of school reform must be to change the institutional governance system and, with it, the massive maldistribution of power and funding in public education.

## PROGRESSIVE FEDERALISM

A cornerstone of the conservative political agenda is to reduce government responsibility for inequality and social need. A major strategy has been the promotion of a "new federalism," which limits the scope of federal intervention and relies on the relative underdevelopment of state government to diminish claims on public services. This latter-day resurrection of "states' rights" is a direct response to the equity role thrust upon the federal government in the 1960s and 1970s. The slashing of federal support for education by 21% between 1980 and 1984, with the sharpest cuts targeting entitlement programs for the disadvantaged, is a clear expression of this strategy.

At the same time, the issues of democratic reform in education suggest that a reordering of intergovernmental relations, a rethinking of the federalist structure, could provide a step forward. Thus, in contrast to the federalism of the New Right, we propose a concept of progressive federalism: expanding the social and fiscal responsibilities of government at all levels—federal, state, and local—and defining the role of each more appropriately to its function.

In our view, progressive federalism affirms that government action is the central instrument for achieving egalitarian goals and more effective practice in public education. Progressive federalism also affirms that the federal government is decisive in establishing national standards of equity, as it has been until recently in the areas of categorical need, school desegregation, and affirmative action. We should continue to use its national scope for these purposes, but be aware that reliance on federal intervention is not sufficient. We need to develop the role of local and state governance as well, to promote more comprehensive responses to educational needs and to engage all levels of government in the struggle for progressive reform. The discussion that follows is, then, a conception of the objectives a movement for democratic schooling could set for the local, state, and federal roles in education.

## LOCAL GOVERNANCE OF LOCAL SCHOOLS

In a system of progressive federalism, the individual school becomes the basic building block in the development of education policy. The local school is the point of service delivery, ultimately responsible for implementing policy, and most directly engaging student and parent needs. Under a decentralized system that promotes local control in schooling, the school site would be the focus of decision-making, determining how broad social and academic goals for schooling are translated into practice.

Any proposal, however, that seeks to establish the local school as the central governance unit in education must contend with the enormous concentration of political and bureaucratic power that has developed in public education over the past century. For many decades, state education aid has provided incentives to consolidate school districts into larger and larger units. Fifty years ago, there were 150,000 school districts across the country; today there are 16,000. With the development of amalgamated and centralized systems, administrative bureaucracies have played ever-expanding roles in prescribing instructional practice and organization and in managing school personnel. Other agencies that are not directly accountable to the public have also proliferated, including testing boards, schools of education, and advocacy organizations. Education is a social service in which expertise has a privileged status. It is also the most extensive bureaucracy and largest employer of any public institution and, as such, provides a power base from which bureaucrats and school authorities have managed formidable resistance to democratic intervention.

Proposals for local governance must also contend with the rise of professionalism as a key element in the public school bureaucracy. With the consolidation of unions and professional associations throughout the educational system, the policy interests of teachers and administrators are expressed chiefly through organizational lobbies. Professional groups have been playing a significant role in determining licensing requirements, instructional standards, job structures, and funding formulas.

This influence is largely felt at the state level, through pressure-group politics within legislatures and departments of education. Professional power-brokering has rarely injected more than narrow self-interest into the policy process. Developing institutional clout has often taken precedence over the hard fights necessary to secure widespread school improvement. The opportunity for frontline educators to build effective popular coalitions with parents, students, and communities has typically been forfeited for influence inside the institutional apparatus. In fact, tactical alliances between professional associations and school authorities have been forged during the past twenty years in continual confrontation with community claims on the schools. Recently, however, there appears to be some slippage in professional and bureaucratic influences in state education policy. The current initiatives for raising requirements and mandating curriculum are coming chiefly from political figures and business leaders, advised by academic experts. It would seem that the business community is currently an active force in state education politics, with professional forces playing the more passive or reactive role.

In theory, popular control in education is balanced against these special interests through the local school board, presumed to be a democratic complement to administrative structures and state legislation. Yet as mechanisms of local control, school boards have also become power centers far removed from the influence of any single community or cohesive voting blocs, especially in heterogeneous rural and urban areas. School boards have tended to represent an area's power elite—the business interests, political machines, upper-middle class civic groups, and established leadership of various subgroups—and often serve as vehicles for their priorities. In highly centralized systems, school boards have come to wield tremendous influence over communities through the allocation of school resources and patronage, while the public they are accountable to is generally fragmented, uninformed, easily divided, and easily demobilized. Elites and school administrators have influence in the district as a whole, while parents and individual schools rarely cross neighborhood lines. Moreover, in both urban and rural systems, district configurations often isolate the groups most in need of school reform. The appointment of school boards in answer to electoral manipulations is hardly a corrective.

The worst, but by no means unique, examples of school

board oligarchy have come to light in school desegregation cases. A recent report in the *Washington Post,* investigating conditions in Georgia public schools, found that, since desegregation was ordered in 1970, schools have been resegregated through the policies of reactionary local boards. Of twenty-two Georgia districts with at least 63% black enrollment, only two had majority black school boards. Forty school boards are still selected by grand juries. The report noted that "school boards presiding over systems with more than 70% black students require 50% less in local property taxes than those with more than 70% white students." In ten years, attendance in the state's private white academies rose from 33,000 to 83,000.[1]

This pattern is not exclusive to the rural South, as Hochschild points out.[2] School district gerrymandering, nonrepresentational election procedures, the manipulation of local taxing mechanisms, the dominance of politicians who are not school parents, the divestiture of public education in the face of integration are practices found throughout the country in varying measures. Ten years ago, the Boston school board was instrumental in inflaming racial conflict to sabotage desegregation orders. In New York City, the massive community mobilization for decentralization was successfully resisted, with token authority granted to community boards, which cover large districts and operate only at the elementary and middle school level. Increased centralization of school decision-making remains the dominant trend throughout the country.

In the face of accrued bureaucratic and political monopolies in local governance, a movement toward re-empowering the local school and diffusing district authority will require a long-term effort. An important ingredient will be altering state aid formulas and mandates to increase the discretionary funding available at the school site, bypassing or at least regulating district control over individual school budgets. Changing the revenue base for school funding is also essential in order to meet equity needs as well as to provide individual schools with viable resources for local management. A major objective should be phasing out the local property tax as the primary base of district revenues. Statewide revenue collection and allocation should then mandate local school equity in per-pupil expenditures and should create additional funds for categorical needs. It may also be time to consider alternative criteria for district formation, which would allow for more voluntary groupings of schools according to need and purpose and which would promote more appropriate and functional economies of scale. We will return to the critical state role in transforming local school and district functions, but should first note the existing models for effective local school governance. We are drawn to the concept of school-site councils, with specific concern for developing new mechanisms to enfranchise low-income and minority communities.

## School-Site Councils

The council idea has developed within initiatives for school-based management, which propose school-based rather than district budgeting, an increase in the discretionary components of the budget, and shared governance among principals, teachers, and parents. In California, school-site councils are a mandated feature of the state's School Improvement Project (SIP), created in 1977 and now operating over half of the state's schools. The program offers sizeable grants to local schools on the basis of an improvement plan designed by a local school council. The council is composed of 50%

parents and community members and 50% staff, including the principal, teachers, and support personnel; in secondary schools, students are also members. Council members are selected by their peers; councils may also draw on other community and school representatives by creating task forces for specific issues. The council conducts an initial assessment of school performance and needs in submitting its improvement plan to the State Department of Education, which prorates the discretionary grant according to the income and performance characteristics of the school. Once a plan is funded, the council is responsible for regularly reviewing the school's instructional programs, designing and implementing improvements, evaluating the results, and replanning appropriately. Preliminary assessments of California's SIP indicate that over 50% of participating schools demonstrated general improvement in school quality, while very few declined.[3]

South Carolina, which instituted local school advisory councils several years ago, has recently upgraded their status with the passage of the 1984 Educational Improvement Act. Every school is mandated to establish a School Improvement Council with parent, community, and teacher representation. The councils have responsibility for issuing an annual report to the state on improvement activities at the school. Incentive grants are available on the basis of the school's gains in achievement, attendance, and parent participation. The Division of Public Accountability in the State Department of Education is promoting the development of the councils and the University of South Carolina College of Education sponsors a technical assistance and training project. In Florida, local school councils and district councils are advisory; they are mandated to participate in the preparation of a school's annual report and may participate in budgeting and planning decisions. In Dade County, school site councils determine the allocation of considerable discretionary funds, and the entire system has shifted to program budgeting and school-based allocations, with computerized information available to each school. In addition to the three state programs for school-site councils, a growing number of urban school districts are developing council models in their school improvement programs.

These early experiments in local governance seem promising, although clearly transitional in terms of granting substantial authority to school community constituents. Ideally, school-site councils would go beyond advisory, planning, and oversight functions to exercise direct decision-making power over budget, personnel, testing and assessment methods, curriculum design, use of the facility, linkages with service and community institutions, and other school improvement priorities. A key aspect is control over line-item budgets, which makes parent and teacher participation more meaningful and more likely to be sustained. Effective councils also require ongoing training programs, exposure to alternative models of schooling, and enlarged technical assistance from the district and state. Another important element is the electoral procedure developed for council membership, which we feel should give parents majority representation and should promote the principle of peer selection for all members. The inclusion of students, community representatives, and local union delegates also strengthens the council's authority.

Our conception of the school council should be distinguished from a parallel development in school-based management, which recognizes the need for local school discretion and accountability, but gives power primarily to local administrators or principals. This orientation arises chiefly from the new emphasis on the principal as an educational leader. Granting new latitude and responsibility to principals may in fact be a positive component in school improvement, but only as part of a broader activation of school constituents. In isolation from other forces, as a management rather than an empowerment strategy, the results will be very uneven and largely contingent on the location and durability of exceptional administrators. The long-run impact of principal-based management strategies seems dubious, given the enormous pull of traditional practice, the magnitude of external pressures on school performance, and the ultimate dependency of local administrators on the bureaucratic power structure for their delegated authority. We are proposing the council strategy because it begins to structurally alter the relationship of the school to the bureaucracy and to district boards, and widens the base of countervailing power.

The school-site council concept is not a panacea; it is a starting point. The council promotes but also relies on sustained parent and community engagement with the school. In some areas, notably depressed areas with highly fluid residence patterns, there may not be a cohesive parent or community infrastructure to turn to. Councils could help develop more community cohesion around the school, but the task would be more difficult than in stable and well-defined neighborhoods. It is clear that sustained parent involvement requires a supportive organizing effort, without which councils would be as vulnerable to political cooptation or professional domination as PTAs and school boards are today.

Moreover, there are potential conflicts in local governance between the priorities and preferences of local communities, on one side, and the principles of equity and effective schooling that develop through a larger social consensus and diverse school experiences. The battles over desegregation amply demonstrate that local communities can be far from enlightened, whether they be small towns in Georgia or the South End in Boston. At the same time, these battles demonstrate that the prior failure to educate and organize around social justice concerns in schooling at the local community level—along with the failure to improve all schools in the course of integration—has made conflicts over desegregation exceedingly bitter and polarized.

Vesting authority in local school councils does not alter the social roots of such conflicts, but it does broaden the locations where they can be addressed and surmounted. Furthermore, vesting authority in local councils cannot exempt communities from meeting standards of school service or from observing legal and civil rights, as the Right envisions in its designs for local control. The concept of progressive federalism includes the necessity of multiple levels of authority, particularly state and federal regulatory functions that safeguard standards and rights.

In sum, the goal of such structural innovation is not to eliminate all problems, but to place these problems in an arena that is accessible to parents and teachers and expressive of community needs, including diversity. Councils that exercise real authority in the local school will not be perfect, but at least the political contests they generate will be meaningful and open to the people with the greatest self-interest in improving school conditions and performance. We believe that the local governance of schools is an indispensable link to effective schooling, and critically important in developing school improvement programs. Local school governance is also a demand with the potential to revitalize the constituencies of public education around democratic values in schooling, in every area of school culture.

## STATE ACTIVISM

For many years, the states have been the weak link in American federalism; today, they offer perhaps the most promising leverage points for change. As many commentators have noted, the new wave of school reform has crystalized a power shift in education policy from the district to the state level. The states have, of course, always been pivotal in education policy, by virtue of their constitutionally mandated authority over schooling. In the past, they have largely delegated this authority, including revenue creation and policy-making, to local school systems. In the last decade, however, states have come to play the largest role in school funding, and state legislatures and education departments are developing an unprecedented role in instructional policy. Politically, the states are also undergoing realignments of voting blocs and constituency groups, with new influence exercised by minorities, women, and single-issue citizens' groups. The old balances of legislative power are changing, reflecting not only the strength of the suburbs, but also shifting urban politics and growing unrest in devastated industrial and rural areas. The states are no longer a political vacuum, but the center stage of educational conflicts in the 1980s.

With such contests developing, it is possible to conceive of the state as an agency for redistributing school resources and control and for mediating the direction of national and local action—roles that progressives have too readily ascribed solely to the federal government. Indeed, it is the hesitation of progressive reformers to grasp the opportunities opening at the state level that most endangers this potential. For as we have noted, conservative and elitist special interests have been active from the start in shaping state responses to the school crisis debate. It is time for progressives to retake the initiative, particularly as the reform impulse moves into programmatic areas.

The current reaction of state governments to new educational responsibilities has spurred both exciting and troubling developments. A positive element of the emerging state role is its increasing fiscal function, and not only as the recipient of block grants under the new federalism. Excluding increases in social security, state spending grew faster than all other government spending in the post-war period. Although state financial conditions are sensitive to economic cycles, state revenue systems and potential revenue sources are greater than they have ever been. Forty states have broad personal income taxes, forty-five have general sales taxes, and forty-five have corporate income taxes. State school aid is a rising percentage of state budgets, now generally about 23%, and twenty-five states reformed their school finance systems during the 1970s. States now fund more than 50% of non-federal school costs and all fifty states have increased education budgets in the past two years.[4] Since 1983, eighteen states have moved to increase teacher salaries and another seventeen states have proposed salary increases in their 1985 legislative sessions; half the states have passed some form of scholarship aid to prospective teachers.[5]

Recently, almost every state has become more comprehensively involved in instructional issues, setting statewide standards and increasing state regulatory controls. State support to education varies widely, but there is clear movement to enlarge their commitments among those states that have historically lagged behind, particularly in the South. Last year, Tennessee, Arkansas, and Mississippi adopted plans to upgrade their minimal state education programs, raise standards, and expand state financing. South Carolina's Educational Improvement Act of 1984 instituted new standards and regulatory mechanisms, improved school finance, and extended school linkages. Texas passed a $2.8 billion Educational Opportunity Act in 1984 and, in early 1985, Georgia passed its Quality Basic Education program, directing $1 billion to the schools over the next three years.[6]

## Standards or Standardization?

We find two disturbing trends, however, in the directions this new state activism is taking. First, only a few states have addressed the local governance needs of schools in their push for school improvement, notably South Carolina with its School Improvement Councils. Prescriptions for change are coming overwhelmingly from the top, prompting the director of the New York School Boards Association to comment about his state's regents, "They're programming every conceivable hour of the day."[7] A second danger in the current activism is that it remains too narrowly centered on the issues that have been promoted by the meritocratic view of school practice. Although there are some departures from the new elitist thrust, the states have yet to take up a broader conception of instructional reform.

A survey conducted by *Education Week* in January 1985 found that policy reform initiatives are overwhelmingly focused on raising quantitative standards. In the last two years, forty-three states have increased high school graduation requirements and five more are considering more stringent requirements this year. Fifteen states now require an exit test for high school graduation, and five more are considering such tests. Thirty-seven states are instituting statewide assessments of student achievement through standardized testing; eight states are using such tests for "promotional gates"; and three more are considering such measures. Twenty-nine states have mandated teacher competency testing, and another ten are considering the idea. Thirty-eight states have enacted, endorsed, or are considering performance-based pay systems for teachers, although most of these plans are still in preliminary stages. Forty-four states are in the process of changing teacher certification requirements. In areas that have more qualitative impacts on learning and teaching conditions, the states have not taken broadscale action. Only thirteen states have acted to limit student/teacher ratios, and only seven states have established some form of pre-school program, with another eight reporting that they are considering such programs.[8]

It should be noted, however, that the focus on more stringent requirements for teachers and students takes on different meanings according to the prior school conditions that each state addresses. In Mississippi, for instance, a grass-roots citizens' campaign joined with state political leadership to enact a reform bill that for the first time created public kindergarten and extended compulsory schooling beyond the third grade. The measure failed to win financing through an oil and gas revenue tax and will be funded by an increase in the sales tax. The Mississippi law is nonetheless an educational and political victory in a state dominated by segregationist school boards and ranking 49th in per-pupil expenditures for education. Mississippi is just embarking on the post-war mission of schooling, with high school entry as an explicit goal.

If the adoption of tougher standards and regulations is advancing the backward southern states into the 1950s, however, it is drawing some of the more advanced states backward toward the '50s. The New York Regents Action Plan, for instance, stiffens curriculum, testing, and promotional requirements, but makes no provision for additional compensatory funding. Given cutbacks in federal and local funding, disadvantaged systems are forced to divert more resources into meeting curricular requirements, with fewer resources directed toward the students most at risk. Furthermore, the neglect of school reorganization issues, gross inequity in the state aid formula, worsening conditions of teacher recruitment, and continued resistance to community involvement mean that qualitative issues of school performance are overwhelmingly ignored. The net result of this approach will be a diminished future for schools in a state where education has been a traditional priority.

States such as Minnesota, Tennessee, California, and Massachusetts, which are now undertaking similar sweeping revisions of standards, should consider these implications: Do new requirements correct existing inequalities in school services to meet all conditions of need? Do new requirements advance more students into all levels of education? Do new requirements improve learning environments so students can *stay* in school—or do they respond only to the call to upgrade skills for the new technical elite?

## Broadening the Agenda

Given the limitations of current state initiatives, we think a constructive posture toward the state role involves three responses: value the potentials of state intervention, challenge the meritocratic assumptions already adopted, and set forth more extensive goals. The key fiscal role played by states in education offers powerful leverage for progressive instructional and institutional change. With some scattered models to draw on, we can envision how state-aid formulas can be reconstructed to achieve the redistribution of resources, to encourage innovative school practices, and to provide incentives for local school governance.

As fiscal agents, states are the appropriate authority for establishing more equitable statewide revenue collection and for distributing funds according to local school needs. We see a four-point agenda for reform in this regard:

1. Local district tax collections for education should be eliminated, reducing differences in resources based on local wealth and property values.

2. State aid formulas should guarantee that all districts, and schools within them, are provided with the same minimum per-pupil expenditures for conducting essential educational services.

3. State funding is also necessary to provide incentive grants for schools to develop programs for school improvement that both raise and extend standards of quality across their enrollment. As in California's SIP, such grant systems should establish different categories of eligibility, according to past school performance and differentials in local resources, mitigating the advantages that privileged schools already exercise in garnering special funds.

4. State funding is necessary for categorical grants to schools based on student disadvantage and special needs. A promising example is offered in Connecticut, where the State Department of Education uses a special fund to improve teacher development in targeted low-income, low-performance schools. In-school programs are being set up to help teachers evaluate school problems and their own roles in school change; in a second phase, the teachers will look at school/community relations.

As we noted earlier, states can also promote school-site

management and local governance practices, both by attaching mandates to funding and by providing technical assistance through state education agencies. States can create grants for local councils and, more generally, can mandate that larger proportions of discretionary funding go to the local schools. States can circumscribe the fiscal authority of districts, mandating school-based budgeting, establishing equity requirements for capital expenditures, and limiting administrative spending. States can provide special funds for implementing decentralization plans.

State education agencies can be an important resource for teacher development, as the Connecticut example shows. The concept of a state-supported teacher corps, covering professional education costs in return for service, is one feasible approach for filling teacher shortage areas, increasing opportunities for poorer students, and increasing service in disadvantaged schools. The National Health Service Corps, now being dismantled under Reagan, was an analogous and effective model. States can also support more extensive in-service training, study grants, and grants given directly to teachers to develop innovative curriculum and programs. Some of these approaches are being tried at the local level, but could readily become more widespread state efforts.

States can mandate a far wider range of instructional improvements than simply raising curriculum or graduation standards. An example is New Jersey's new requirement that districts provide free and appropriate pre-school programs for children with handicapping conditions—in effect, it is a special education Head Start program, operated through the schools. The example also illustrates the necessary state role in combating discrimination and segregation, particularly the forms of "second-generation" segregation that develop within school programs through tracking and place-ment practices. In addition, state action is particularly well suited to experimental programs, since local systems hesi-tate to risk their scarce resources on untested approaches. Such projects could include developing community-based programs for reducing class size, introducing community service components in secondary education, and designing qualitative instruments for student assessment.

The potential for states to move beyond school regulation to a broadly redistributive role in funding and governance, and a leadership role in restructuring school practice, is greater than ever before. The fulfillment of this potential de-mands, however, that reform advocates and constituencies also enlarge their focus beyond city and federal politics to in-clude the state arena. Community organizations and citizen coalitions are just beginning to appreciate the new arena for action that state government represents. Since regressive in-terests also sense this potential, it becomes all the more im-perative to engage the gubernatorial, legislative, and bureau-cratic structures of state power.

## FEDERAL RESPONSIBILITY

The significant entry of the federal government into educa-tion is relatively recent, initiated by the *Brown* decision, the Civil Rights Act of 1964, and the Elementary and Secondary Education Act of 1965. The federal role was the product of long and difficult struggle by social movements to break through the deadlocked politics of regressive state legis-latures and urban political machines. Federal programs cen-tered on entitlements that were intended to be compensatory and redistributive and on sanctions against civil rights abuse. Although federal intervention did not confront the basic issues of school governance, it did establish peripheral mechanisms, such as the parent advisory requirements attached to the entitlement programs.

Reagan's success in divesting federal responsibility for education is not a reason for abandoning the federal arena. The federal government is the only feasible agency for the redistribution of wealth on a nationwide basis, both in its tax policies and in its priorities for public spending. The federal government is also the primary agent for promoting geographic as well as individual equity. In setting objectives for a renewed federal role, we not only should seek to restore the entitlement function and categorical funding but should also extend the interrelation of federal and state activity.

The federal government can play a leading role in setting equity standards for state and local school authorities, through mandates attached to federal aid. If federal highway money can be made contingent on the states' enacting a drinking age of twenty-one, federal education dollars can become contingent on revising state aid formulas to equalize basic per-pupil expenditures. Both legal sanctions against discriminatory fiscal practice and grants that support the state redistributive role can be implemented.

Moreover, federal allocations can include incentives for the decentralization of school governance and for improving the mainstreaming goals of categorical programs. The federal government has a special role to play in developing and expanding community-based educational programs, such as early childhood education, public service employment projects for youth, drop-out prevention services, literacy services, and the many other school/community linkages recommended in this book. The federal government has an important impact on school and student expectations through the student aid for higher education it makes available.

The federal government has a continuing and fundamental responsibility to redress the educational effects of racial and sexual discrimination, as well as discrimination based on economic status, native language, national origin, religion, and handicapping conditions. In our view, racial polarization, which is closely linked to economic and sexual inequity, is the most acute problem confronting this society and our education system. While the subversion of desegregation efforts has prompted many to question whether mandated desegregation should or can be a vehicle for racial equality, the case is not closed as far as we are concerned. We agree with Hochschild that there is ample evidence that desegregation can succeed: "We don't need a lot of 'new ideas.' What we do need is a willingness to learn the right lessons from the last thirty years and to recognize that desegregation need not fail."[9] Clearly, the priority of desegregation as a mechanism for achieving greater equality should be determined not by those who enjoy the privileges of discrimination, but by those who are victimized by it.

Furthermore, federal responsibility for combating discrimination is not conveniently absolved with the eclipse of desegregation, or by the judicial retreat on affirmative action. An agenda for democratic education must include a strong, interventionist federal role in both prohibiting discrimination and providing corrective resources. This interventionist role clearly requires a challenge to the prevailing philosophy of the executive branch, as well as a demand for legislative initiative in Congress. In addition to discriminatory school funding practices, areas needing immediate attention include non-compliance with bilingual and special education mandates, teacher recruitment and promotion, exclusionary discipline, student misclassification, and enrollment patterns in selective admissions schools or programs (particularly vocational, magnet, and gifted programs).

## PUBLIC OWNERSHIP IN EDUCATION

Progressive federalism seeks to broaden citizen participation at all levels of government, as both a cause and an effect of school change. Progressive federalism denies past liberal assumptions that reform can only be achieved at the national level through the enforcement of uniform policies and practices. And it denies the conservative thrust toward state government control at the expense of federal support and the local control of schools.

Central to the success of progressive reform, and progressive federalism as an alternative approach to governance, is the concept of public ownership in education. Public ownership means government responsibility for maintaining school institutions financially and administratively, under constitutional principles. But public ownership also means access and participation by citizens. It means a democratic process guiding the governance process, which goes beyond the election of school boards or public officials.

Some would argue, implicitly, that the democratic process is too imperfect, contentious, or unreliable a mechanism to be trusted with responsibility for the conduct of education. It is certainly true that democratic processes, and citizen involvement, are often manipulated, since not all participants have equal resources with which to exercise influence. It is also true that the citizen majority at any given time or place can be ignorant, intolerant, myopic, or misdirected. It is true that democratic mechanisms can be mere formalities, giving the illusion of citizen control while power accumulates in the hands of elites and bureaucrats. For all of these possibilities, there is no short cut and no purpose in retreat. If we seek a democratic mission for schooling, we have to confront the limits of our democratic capacities and push them back. We have to construct better opportunities for citizen action, as well as citizen education. We cannot achieve public responsibility without empowering the public. We cannot achieve public ownership if we do not fight over whose interests and agendas are already setting education policy.

A more challenging argument against this vision is made by those who feel that democratic school reforms will not make any difference. In this view, school outcomes cannot be dramatically changed without more sweeping systemic changes in economic and social structures. The argument has some validity. Schools are deeply affected by conditions of inequality and stratification that prevail in society at large. These conditions not only create barriers to school improvement but limit the impact of improvement where it is achieved. Unemployment rates of over 50% still await ghetto youth, whether they have graduated from high school or not, and certainly offer no incentive to graduate.

Yet we believe that schools, because they can belong to the citizens they serve and not to the marketplace, have the potential to be more than a mirror reflection of social injustice. When citizens claim ownership of education, schools can become countervailing institutions directed by democratic purposes. All children can learn, and learn more than we are now teaching them about the value of knowledge. If all children's economic or social needs are not being met, schools can at least address their human needs for mastery and skill, for thought and communication, for awareness and activity, for self-esteem and shared respect. If all children are not equally rewarded for learning, they can at least be equally prepared to contend with unfair realities and even to change them.

This is not to say that public ownership, in its fullest sense, will eliminate the historic tension between democratic and elitist missions of schooling. Indeed, this tension is likely to intensify with each step toward citizen involvement, since vested interests do not yield easily, and since the citizens themselves are torn between ideals and expediency. But progress can be sustained and meaningful if schools are seen as appropriate and necessary arenas for defining and asserting the public interest. On this issue, the current debate over school reform is critical in its own right. Beyond the immediate policy outcomes, the debate is pivotal to restoring public recognition that public institutions can meet human needs and should extend human rights, including the right to learn.

In today's political climate, it may seem hard to counter the prevailing tide of private interest and competitive gain with notions of public ownership and social responsibility. Public education clearly has not escaped the broader trend to dismantle public services, circumvent equity mechanisms, and lower expectations. Yet most Americans still value public schooling as a fundamental entitlement and an essential expression of citizenship and community. As such, public education becomes all the more important terrain for defending the public sector and re-establishing social priorities.

It may be that for some time progressive advances on this terrain will seem small and scattered. But in school buildings, in neighborhoods, in statehouses and national forums, the school reform debate is mobilizing new energies and provoking renewed commitments to the democratic vision of public education. If the first round of this decade's school debate has gone to the new elitists, the coming rounds will be more vigorously contested.

# 7.

## Building a New Agenda

This book has surveyed a broad range of issues that are important to progressive directions in school change. We have tried to treat the subject comprehensively, with the sense that we must grasp the whole even while we address its distinct parts, we must have a long view even while we take small steps. We want to stress that isolated reforms, adjusting one or another aspect of the education system, will not go far in altering the instructional environment or institutional politics of schooling. Yet we are not suggesting that solutions can only be pursued in an all-or-nothing fashion. Rather, we suggest that any design for school improvement should lead us to ask: Does the proposal treat the symptom or the disease—does it locate the problem in individual or in institutional performance? Does it assume a hierarchy of merit or recognize that schools must teach all children according to their needs? Does it narrow our goals for achievement or broaden our concepts of what students can and should learn in order to function in society? We must also ask: Does a given reform pre-empt the empowerment of school constituents or enlarge their capacity to shape school policy and practice? Does it lower expectations for students and for schools or raise expectations and demands? Does it reinforce elitist goals for education or advance the democratic school mission?

In terms of what to do tomorrow, there are a number of immediate policy issues that call for alternative responses. We have argued throughout the book that most current reform initiatives can be framed in ways that either support or undermine the spirit of democratic schooling. For the most part, today's popular reforms are put forward as universally beneficial panaceas, while in practice they function as elitist prescriptions. Struggles around reform designs can alter this direction and change the focus of public concern.

One example is the merit pay concept, which is being constructed largely as a competitive mechanism for teacher motivation, but could be reconstructed as a fund to reward collective efforts for school improvement and to support collaborative teacher development programs. Another example is school-based management, which can be utilized to increase the authority of local administrators or can be a vehicle for teacher and parent empowerment as well. Business partnerships, which are now the central strategy for school-to-work linkages, raise serious questions of creaming, vocational tracking, and corporate intervention in public education. But school partnerships can be broadened to focus on a diverse range of community activities, including public services, which strengthen the school as a community institution.

The issues of standards—curriculum, time, and testing—are most often raised in quantitative terms, with the call for "more" opposed to the notion of "less." But standards should be concerned with quality, with setting goals for school performance without rigidly dictating teaching approaches or rigidly labeling students. There are similar dual approaches to entitlement programs, which too often end up as mechanisms for segregating and stigmatizing special needs students, but can be designed to redress social inequities, introduce more innovative and individualized teaching practices, and offer new resources to mainstream education.

We have also pointed out two sides of the voucher or optional enrollment issue. Where option systems function as open markets with scarce resources, all students will not have an equal or comparable range of choices and the results will be a greater stratification of schools and students. Where option systems are constructed to add resources to deficient schools and to accommodate equally all levels of need—and where they are accessible to parent and community involvement—they may well promote diversity and responsiveness. In another example, the Effective Schools movement illustrates the dual potentials of a school improvement methodology that, if imposed as a static prescription, will have minimal impact but, if pursued through a participatory and collaborative process, can make enduring changes in the learning environment.

Any programmatic issue can reproduce the tension between democratic and elitist approaches, posing choices of design and implementation that serve either tendency. Certainly, there are structural reforms that are more conducive to democratic or to elitist goals; and there are different priorities in each agenda. But when we look at the issues, whether in response to the neo-conservative agenda or in advancing our own, the critical questions are not just about intentions or objectives. We must also evaluate the institutional structures and political processes that any given reform will operate within or will itself generate. These are the qualitative issues, implicit in any concrete program, which this book has attempted to draw out and debate. In doing so, we have come to a number of conclusions that we feel represent the case for democratic schooling:

1. The crisis of achievement in American education is twofold: there is a crisis of inequality and a crisis of citizenship. Our primary concern should lie with the acute failure to provide a vast number of low-income and minority students with decent schools and skills. We also need to recognize a chronic failure to enhance all children's capacities to think critically and to acquire social knowledge.

2. Massive school failure is primarily the long-term consequence of meritocratic school practices, which have created distinctly different conditions in elite and mass education. Moreover, meritocracy rationalizes school failure by attributing it to individual deficiencies, rather than to schools that do not serve children well. Today, as in the past, school resources, expectations, and services are highly unequal, both absolutely and relative to student needs. Competitive standards and methods of achievement compound social and educational advantages and disadvantages, and force unfair trade-offs between different kinds of need. Our school system has thus reproduced the prevailing pattern of social stratification, not transcended it.

3. Today's schools are not suffering an erosion of quality due to excessive egalitarian reform: the problem is not that schools have shortchanged those on the top, but that schools have so completely underserved those on the bottom. Overall, the equity reforms of the 1960s and 1970s accomplished a shift from exclusive meritocracy, which shut many students out, to inclusive meritocracy, which granted students access but not the resources to achieve. In the 1980s, even inclusion is being undermined, as elitist get-tough prescrip-

tions erect new barriers and push more students out of school.

4. Economic realities do not justify the claim that a more competitive school regime will raise productivity and widely enhance job opportunities. The growing polarization of the workforce into a small professional strata and a large pool of low-wage, de-skilled service and production workers indicates that education will mean more for a few and less for many, in terms of economic reward. The logic of today's marketplace is to lower expectations and limit chances for the majority of children, and elitist schooling reinforces this logic.

5. Schools do not have to mirror economic imperatives; they can also respond to social imperatives. If education were constructed around the social needs of children, families, communities, and a democratic society, the priority would be to endow all children with the basic and higher-order skills needed to fulfill personal and citizenship roles. The mission of schooling would be individual and social empowerment, which itself would promote more equitable chances of survival in the labor market. We believe schools can make a difference in our quality of life, but realizing this potential will require different schools.

6. School improvement and effective instruction cannot be legislated by quantitatively raising requirements, by imposing reward-and-punish systems of performance, or by singling out aspects of school practice that can be technically manipulated. More of the same is not better, when traditional practice has contributed to both school failure and alienation. Successful approaches to improving performance recognize the need to qualitatively change the environmental context—the school culture—that conditions the learning process. Effective reform must be multi-dimensional,

must address structural, organizational, and managerial issues, and must account for the quality of relationships among staff and students.

7. In the debate over instructional reform, the differences between democratic and elitist approaches to improving instruction cannot be reduced to false choices between permissiveness and authority, or low and high standards. The differences represent conflicts over what constitutes achievement and who should achieve. These conflicts are expressed in general terms as the opposition between universal or selective access; between inclusive or exclusive advancement; between supportive or punitive motivation; between cooperative or competitive achievement; between collaborative or hierarchic management; between bottom-up and top-down change processes.

8. The approaches that constitute democratic education are known to promote school improvement in deprived and deficient schools; they can also work to make all schools more engaging, more attuned to individual potential, more collectively rewarding. Likewise, the conditions of educational achievement found in advantaged schools—such as better staffing ratios, greater community accountability, more resources for enrichment and supportive services—are conditions that can be provided in all schools. Equality does not dictate mediocrity any more than quality depends on privilege. Since we know a great deal about what makes all kinds of schools more effective, the issue is why we use that knowledge for some and not all children.

9. Addressing the crises in public education thus necessitates a challenge to the priorities we have set and to the way we set priorities. Progressive change must include reforming the political processes that determine our choices, both

within the institution and in government. Today, the grass-roots constituents of education—parents, teachers, community members—are increasingly distanced from the centers of power. As in other social institutions, control over school policy and practice is concentrated in the hands of administrative and professional bureaucrats, special interests, and political elites.

10. Progressive reform therefore requires empowering the constituents of schooling as both essential elements of school culture and indispensable agents for change. Progressive reform also requires renewing our conception of the school as a community institution, both drawing on and adding to community resources. The conception that schools should be socially responsive does not detract from their primary function of instruction; on the contrary, schools must respond to the societal conditions that influence them in order to perform well for all students.

11. Promoting constituent activism around school needs both generates and requires new power relationships. In advocating the construction of progressive federalism in education, we are calling for all levels of government to play a redistributive role in regard to governance as well as funding. The local governance of local schools is a core issue of school improvement and constituent empowerment, but will occur only with major policy shifts at the state level, an arena of education politics where progressives must direct new energy. Locating basic decision-making power at the school site also means that power-sharing mechanisms and equity standards must be more, not less, rigorously promoted at the state and federal levels. Alongside the policy goals of progressive federalism, it is necessary to renew our national sense of public ownership in education, defending

schools as public institutions through which citizens rightfully assert social needs and priorities for their children and communities.

There is one more argument to add to these conclusions and to our debate with the new elitists. The emphasis they place on standardization and technique has been used on occasion to imply that financial resources are not at the heart of the school crisis, except perhaps in regard to teacher pay and shortages. Yet nearly every progressive measure that we have identified requires a higher level of fiscal support, as well as a redistribution of funding to those who are currently underserved. If the majority of American school children cannot rely on either meritocracy or the marketplace to secure their right to productive knowledge, if education can only advance through its democratic mission, then we have far to go in fulfilling our commitments. Democratic education can be pursued, but it cannot be achieved without substantially increasing funding to education—funding for equity, for innovation, for participatory institutions linked to community and social needs. Money is never a solution, but it is an essential means to an end. To those who argue that equality of results simply costs too much, Tom Bethell offers the best reply: "Compared to what?"[1]

## CITIZENS' MOVEMENTS FOR DEMOCRATIC SCHOOLING

In concluding our conception of democratic directions for school reform, we stress again the essential role that citizens' movements in education must play in deciding the choices confronting us. These movements are only at formative stages today, redefining their vision and searching for entry points in the political process. As this work proceeds across the country, a number of promising approaches have emerged, some of which we cite here.

## Washington, D.C.: Parents United for Full Public School Funding

Parents United is both a grassroots parent organization and a policy advocacy group working to defend public education resources and promote school improvement in the District of Columbia. It was organized in 1980 as a response to drastic cutbacks in the District's school budget, which included the loss of nearly one-tenth of the teaching staff. Parents United had an immediate base of parent support in predominantly poor, black areas of Washington, where inner-city schools have suffered all too typical problems of decay, overcrowding, and deficient services. The organization also mobilized parents and citizens from more advantaged areas who were alarmed by the financial crisis and inequities throughout the school system.

During its first two years, Parents United developed a public campaign to restore school funding and staffing, relying on the volunteer efforts of parents and educators. The organization was able to generate highly visible community concern and this activism, combined with its comprehensive analysis of the school budget, led to major funding increases in 1982–84 and the recovery of many of the programs cut in 1980.

Parents United has since created a membership base of approximately 1,000 parents in eighty local schools; in addition, forty-seven local schools are affiliated with the organization. Its grassroots activity focuses on school improvement, helping parents to monitor school performance and to develop partnerships with educators in meeting school needs. Parents United has also established the Washington Parent Group Fund, a foundation to sponsor special enrichment projects initiated in local schools, sustained through parent-fundraising and matching private donations. Concerned that District policy address both excellence and equity, Parents United has recently developed a seventeen-point report that advocates systemwide reforms in teacher quality, special programs, administrative costs, school building usage, and custodial services. The organization maintains a very small staff, continuing to utilize volunteer services to enhance its organizing work and its increasingly sophisticated research capacity.

In addition to school practice concerns, the organization has taken on political issues in education that parent groups have traditionally found difficult to address. In 1981, Parents United played a leading role in defeating a districtwide tuition tax credit initiative by a voter margin of nine to one. In 1982, Parents United developed a widely publicized study of a contract dispute between the teachers' union and the D.C. Board of Education; the report was instrumental in resolving the impasse and its primary recommendations were adopted in the settlement.

Parents United is a model for citizen involvement in education that offers the potential to initiate as well as react to school performance issues. It has helped a deeply troubled urban school system survive and surmount fiscal crisis and, in the process, created a civic coalition in support of public education. Perhaps more uniquely, it has also created a broad-based activist constituency with ties to the local schools and commitments to school equality. Pressing problems remain in the D.C. public schools and educational resources lag far behind needs, but Parents United represents a vehicle for participation and change that could not have been generated without citizen action.

## Chicago: Designs for Change/Chicago Schoolwatch

Designs for Change was founded in 1977 by independent education activists as a child advocacy and research organization with primary concern for improving Chicago public schools. The organization's investigations of school performance have identified critical failures in the school system, particularly for black and Latino communities, which in turn prompted the formation of Chicago Schoolwatch, a citywide parent organizing project.

Since 1983, Chicago Schoolwatch has organized in six of the city's twenty school districts, using *All Our Kids Can Learn to Read*, a curriculum based on school effectiveness research and on evaluations developed by Designs for Change. Through the Schoolwatch campaign, parent groups have examined their schools' performance indicators, assessed school strengths and weaknesses, developed school improvement plans, and pressured school authorities for necessary policy changes at the school, district, and municipal level. At a citywide conference in 1985, Schoolwatch also demonstrated legislative support for a statewide Urban School Improvement Act, developed by the organization to meet the policy demands of its parent groups.

Complementing Schoolwatch activism, Designs for Change has been a critical source of information, analysis, and policy recommendations in Chicago, where the school system is not noted for the quality of its research, its openness to scrutiny, or its commitment to minority constituents. In 1982, Designs published *Caught in the Web*, documenting the massive over-referral of black students to classes for the mentally retarded. As a result of that study and a lawsuit brought by Designs for Change, the school system was forced to change its referral policies and to retest and reclassify more than 10,000 black students previously assigned to special education. *The Bottom Line,* issued in 1985, documented Chicago's extremely high drop-out rate and demonstrated that only a fraction of students graduating from inner-city high schools can read at or above grade level. This study prompted the Chicago Board of Education and the new superintendent of schools to replace the Chicago Mastery Learning program, which had unsuccessfully structured the teaching of reading throughout the system.

This work has also brought citywide attention to educational needs in Chicago, contributing to the movement to elect Harold Washington as mayor. The Washington campaign enlisted staff members from Designs for Change to develop an education platform; since taking office, Mayor Washington has consistently supported Designs for Change initiatives. In addition, Designs for Change has played a pivotal role in organizing the Illinois Fair Schools Coalition, which unites educational advocacy and youth service groups to promote state legislation and policy reform to improve schooling for underserved students. The Urban School Improvement Act is now a centerpiece of these efforts. Finally, Designs for Change has contributed to the development of parallel advocacy organizations nationwide. Its 1983 study, *Child Advocacy and the Schools,* defines a range of principles underlying successful practice among local, state, and national advocacy groups.

Designs for Change demonstrates the impact that independent monitoring and analysis can have in targeting strategic leverage points for school reform. This impact derives not only from the caliber of its research, but also from the linkage of research to grassroots campaigns for school improvement, and the linkage of education activism to multi-issue movements for new municipal and state priorities.

## Seattle: Citizens Education Center Northwest

The Citizens Education Center was first established in 1976 as the Citizens for Fair School Funding, an ad hoc citizens' group that focused on inequities in school finance that had persistently shortchanged urban and low-income school communities. Due in part to their efforts, Washington State has substantially revised its education funding formulas, with the state now providing 75% of local school funding. In 1979, the group reorganized as an advocacy and organizing center committed to monitoring school finance and developing a wider range of school improvement policies, both for Seattle and for the state.

Seattle's public schools rate high on national performance indicators, but the averages mask wide disparities in school quality and some classic problems of urban schooling, including teacher demoralization and a lack of consistent, strategic leadership from the administration and school board. Seattle is also a city in demographic transition, with the minority population of blacks, Asians, and Latinos now reaching 50%; racial tensions are a persistent undercurrent in school politics and minorities are highly underrepresented in school policy-making and service.

The Center's first major campaign, Project ACCESS, sought to deal with the need for new representation and leadership mechanisms by introducing school-site council concepts to the Seattle district. Project ACCESS (A Community Cooperating for Effective Seattle Schools) operated from 1981 to 1985 at two levels. The first level of work was to lay a foundation for parent involvement in local schools, so that effective councils could evolve. After conducting a survey of parents, community members, and school personnel on how they viewed school performance and school-home relations, the Project targeted twelve elementary and middle schools that served primarily low-income families and had little prior parent involvement. The Project organized parent volunteers to work in these schools and increased school contacts with students' homes. Each of these schools now has an identifiable parent constituency, four have consolidated active parent groups, and one has formed an advisory council with parents, teachers, and administrators. The Project's report, *Parents as Partners*, offers insights learned from this experience.

The second level of work was to influence the district to adopt a team concept for local school decision-making, which became policy in 1984. Although the implementation of the team approach has been uneven, and parent representation on the teams has not been universally accepted, the policy represents an opening for continuing efforts to establish both school-based management and parent participation structures. In the process, the Center has become a key actor in a coalition of progressive groups seeking to realign school board politics.

Recognizing that state legislation could also play a role in fostering the council concept, the Center spearheaded the enactment of a pilot program for school-based management in 1985. The statewide program provides funding to selected schools seeking to set up local governance councils, with parent participation, along the lines of similar programs already operative in California and South Carolina. The Center is working with the state to implement the program and will help the designated schools to organize parent involvement.

The school-based management bill is part of a larger package of legislative reforms that the Center has formulated through its statewide Education Campaign, launched in 1984 to act on rising public concerns over school performance and sponsored by fourteen public interest organizations. The effort again has a two-pronged focus, to involve local communities in setting educational priorities and to organize a leadership coalition behind a reform agenda. The Campaign held public meetings in seventeen cities and towns across the state to inform citizens about school improvement needs, with particular attention to equity issues and to minority communities that have previously been excluded from the debate. It also convened the Education Leadership Group, bringing together for the first time leaders from the teachers' union, community organizations, civic coalitions, and the state's Business Roundtable.

What had promised to be a sweeping reform bill in 1985 was sidelined by a major state budget shortfall, but pieces of the package were enacted, including an early childhood education bill for low-income pre-schoolers. Despite these limited gains, the effort has created new support for public education and new vehicles for continued pressure on the state.

The Center's experience with Project ACCESS and its Education Campaign indicate the importance of having an organizational base for sustaining citizens' initiatives. These initiatives will inevitably encounter fiscal constraints, administrative inertia, and special interest resistance, even where the political climate is generally favorable to public education. What is critical to the Center's approach, and the long-term outcome for school reform, is its capacity to connect with the grassroots constituencies with the greatest need for school improvement and to build step-by-step bridges to their policy goals.

New Jersey: Institute for Citizen Involvement in Education

The Institute was established in 1984 by New Jersey Schoolwatch, an advocacy coalition of citizens' and business groups that, for nearly a decade, has promoted responsive education in the state's declining urban, industrial districts. The Institute's work addresses two specific needs that emerged from Schoolwatch efforts. The first was to rebuild a core of skilled parent and citizen activists to lead local school improvement campaigns. Schoolwatch had found that much of the parent activism that had developed in low-income and minority communities in the late 1960s and early 1970s had been eroded by school funding cutbacks, hostility and indifference from school officials, increased economic stress, and a general climate of retrenchment. The second need was to provide local activists with high-level training and educational opportunity that would contribute to their personal development and their sustained involvement in school issues.

To meet these needs, the Institute designed the Public Policy and Public Schools program, an accredited, entry-level college course, now being given to parents and school activists in fifteen districts across the state. At each location, the course is held in non-traditional community settings, including local school classrooms. Meeting in twenty-four sessions, the course utilizes Effective Schools research findings to discuss the legal, financial, and administrative structures of public education; curriculum, instruction, and testing; school climate and discipline; school and district management; school improvement strategies; and parent participation. In addition, Effective Schools research methods are used to investigate the performance of the local schools in the district where the course is held. The program's instructors are recruited from the ranks of parent organizers and education advocates associated with Schoolwatch over the past decade.

By mid-1985, some 425 students, mostly low-income minority women, had completed the course. They represent a new generation of skilled local activists, both for school improvement and for community organizing. In at least two districts, the program has generated leadership for community campaigns to alter the balance of power on district school boards.

In Plainfield, New Jersey, a dormant school reform organization, the Plainfield Education Study Team (PEST), was revived through the Public Policy and Public Schools class. PEST developed an educational position paper for the district, started an organizing drive to expand its membership, and moved to make school board members elected rather than appointed. PEST succeeded in placing the issue on the city ballot and organized a favorable voter turnout. During the following school board election, PEST mounted a fundraising and canvassing campaign for a slate of four candidates, three of whom won school board seats. This activity is continuing around the upcoming school board election.

In Newark, an Institute instructor became the key organizer for People United for Better Schools (PUBS), a coalition of parent and neighborhood groups, local churches, and the school employee unions representing teachers, cafeteria workers, and custodians. Like PEST, PUBS challenged the traditional political arrangements, which had placed control of the school system in the mayor's office, by calling for an elected school board and winning a citywide referendum on the issue. In two subsequent school board elections, PUBS achieved a solid majority and won control of the Newark school board. The Institute instructor and several graduates of its program played central roles in this transformation of school governance.

Both PEST and PUBS now face the more difficult task of translating electoral victory into comprehensive, community-based school improvement. In Plainfield, there is a clear need to create accountability mechanisms that keep the school board members elected by PEST responsive to its educational program. In Newark, the task is to formulate and implement a concrete reform agenda that can continue to engage the parent and neighborhood base activated by PUBS. Without that agenda and renewed ties to the grassroots components of the coalition, power will gravitate toward the more organized forces, particularly the school employee unions, and the reform impulse could easily be displaced by new school elites and new systems of patronage.

These electoral initiatives indicate the potential for citizen action to open up the school governance process and to produce new opportunities for programmatic reform, even if success in gaining power poses a new set of problems in exercising it. Moreover, the PEST and PUBS examples demonstrate the potential of the Institute's parent education program to stimulate new leadership and vision for school reform. Soon the program will have almost a thousand graduates in urban areas throughout New Jersey. This not only represents a supportive network for district-level reform, but also a substantial base for launching a statewide advocacy coalition to influence legislative and administrative action on urban school issues.

## National: People for the American Way—Freedom to Learn Program

People for the American Way (PFAW) is a national citizens' organization promoting democratic rights and values in civic affairs. It was formed in 1980 by prominent leaders from the public and private sectors who were concerned about the climate of intolerance that accompanied the political successes of the New Right; the organization now has 200,000 members nationwide. One component of its work is the Freedom to Learn program, organized in 1982 to counter a mounting trend toward academic censorship based on political, religious, racial, and sexual biases.

The program's main focus has been a textbook review project, investigating the impact of rightwing campaigns against "secular humanism" on textbook publishers. Initial studies found that an alarming range of publishers had not only systematically eliminated or watered down controversial topics but were also lowering the comprehension level of their texts and expurgating or abridging the classics. The program also found that school authorities charged with adopting textbooks were widely uninformed on the subject matter they reviewed; many uncritically accepted whatever publishers offered or were unduly influenced by censorship pressure groups.

In response, the Freedom to Learn program convened a national conference of educational, religious, and civic groups in 1983 specifically to address the treatment of evolution in science curricula and textbooks. The conference generated an important test case on evolution teaching the following year in Texas. The Texas Board of Education had long maintained an anti-evolution guideline for biology textbook selection. The staff of the Freedom to Learn program organized a statewide petition campaign to reverse the board's policy and initiated a court action that successfully repealed the guideline. The program then reviewed the available textbooks with the help of local educators and scientists to better inform the board's advisory panel.

This work developed into *A Consumers' Guide to Biology Textbooks*, published in 1985 and widely disseminated. The guide had an important impact on the recent decision by California's state superintendent of education to reject all junior high biology textbooks submitted by publishers for use in the state, because of their consistently inadequate treatment of evolution. The Freedom to Learn program is now undertaking a similar review of history textbooks, in collaboration with scholars and educators, that will focus on the treatment of controversial topics such as the Bill of Rights and the heritage of American pluralism.

In addition, the Freedom to Learn program is expanding its direct organizing by forming Community Action Teams to work with local citizens' groups confronting censorship issues. Few of these cases receive national attention, but there are hundreds of communities across the country—especially in rural areas—where school boards, administrators, teachers, and librarians are under political and even judicial attack for refusing to concede to censorship demands. The Freedom to Learn program is developing a national network of community activists to share information, strategies, and successful practice in countering these attacks; it has already published a useful organizing manual, *Protecting the Freedom to Learn: A Citizen's Guide*. The program is also developing media resources, locally and nationally, to broaden public awareness of censorship efforts and the threat they pose to academic freedom and quality education.

The Freedom to Learn program is an example of a policy initiative that has become effective by engaging public controversy rather than retreating from it. It is also another example of the importance of linking advocacy expertise to citizen involvement and of integrating national, state, and local levels of activism. By challenging the censorship movement, and particularly the tendency toward self-censorship that it fosters through intimidation, People for the American Way has helped to revive commitments to open and informed inquiry as a principle of public schooling.

## LOOKING AHEAD

These five examples of citizens' movements in education tell only part of the story. We have cited groups that have grown from small cores of education advocates, often professionals, to become vehicles for community-based organizing and civic coalitions. These groups function chiefly in urban settings and rely on substantial funding from private foundations to maintain offices and staff. While such groups may currently represent the most coherent, consolidated organizations around progressive school policy and practice, there are many more varieties and levels of activism for democratic school reform.

There are countless community, parent, and teacher groups engaged in intense struggles around schooling. These localized campaigns identify a wide range of concerns about quality and equality, representation and participation, that can spark citizen action and create new constituencies for reform. Across the country, struggles are being waged against regressive school boards, against the dismantling of entitlement programs, against discriminatory discipline, against punitive testing and tracking, and against many other barriers to educational equity. Struggles are being waged for early childhood programs, for the appointment of new school administrators, for a school bond issue or tax allocation, for the survival of the local schoolhouse, for academic freedom, and a host of other needs.

Some of these grassroots efforts receive supportive resources, such as legal assistance or organizer training; many are on their own. Some of these efforts represent passing campaigns; others are the work of ongoing organizations. Some are initiated by multi-issue citizens' groups, where school improvement is part of a larger social justice agenda. Some school struggles launch those broader organizations and agendas. It is clear, however, that too many school reform initiatives at the community level are not well connected to parallel struggles in other communities, states, and regions. And there is not yet an overarching national movement expressing the vitality and urgency of citizen demands for democratic education.

A critical step forward will be the creation of new alliances among school constituencies at state and local levels—alliances that draw together parents, frontline educators, community activists, and education advocates. The potential for grassroots alliances is based on profound common interests in better conditions for schooling, but realizing this potential will require each constituency to overcome a regrettable history of isolation and misplaced blame. A further necessary step will be linking educational alliances to broader political movements and reasserting the priority of public education as an empowerment issue.

Prospects for the renewal of progressive coalition politics

are emerging, even as conditions of inequality grow more extreme. Opportunities to develop an education agenda exist in the vast network of community organizing that has taken root over the past decade. Opportunities exist in the growing electoral participation of minorities and women, in the shifting alignments of urban politics, in embryonic "rainbow" alliances. There is new opportunity in the emergence of citizens' coalitions deeply engaged in state legislative politics and beginning to influence issues such as environmental protection, tax reform, consumer rights, and economic development. And there are opportunities on the national level, with the coalescence of social movements against federal cutbacks, such as the unprecedented effort mounted to save Chapter 1 and Head Start funding.

The revival of a public education movement may be aided by fresh analysis of the many complex issues of schooling, but finally a renewed movement will develop from concern that generates activism and activism that generates new vehicles and strategies for struggle, new expectations and visions for the school mission. If we accept that reform is a demanding process, which cannot be advanced through technocratic formulas or token commitments, then we have already gotten past what the meritocrats are telling us about school change.

Every American has a stake in the success of public education as a universal right and a social institution. Schools are part of the promise of a democratic society because schools are capable of endowing all our children with the knowledge and reason to function as fully enfranchised citizens. Schools are part of the promise of a democratic society because they belong to the people they serve and can be directed to meet their needs. The persistence of unequal resources and narrow achievement in today's schools tells us that education must contend with powerful forces of economic stratification and social injustice. But this reality also signals the potential importance of schools as countervailing public institutions, as correctives for inequality, and as springboards for social change.

The opportunities now before us to reform education are also opportunities to recover democratic aspirations and prepare ourselves and our children to build a more decent society. The necessity of democratic reform lies in the millions of lives diminished and the millions of dreams deferred by continuing school failure. The possibility of democratic reform lies with citizens who choose equality as the standard of social progress and the measure of their own empowerment.

# Notes

## Chapter 2: The Mission of Schooling

1. Heritage Foundation cited in Fred L. Pincus, "From Equity to Excellence: The Rebirth of Educational Conservatism," *Social Policy*, Winter 1984, p. 51.
2. *Toward More Local Control: Financial Reform in Public Education*, final report of the Advisory Panel on Financing Elementary and Secondary Education (Marshner Commission) (Washington, D.C.: U.S. Department of Education, December 1982).
3. William J. Bennett, U.S. Secretary of Education, in a letter introducing the Equity and Choice Act of 1985 (TEACH) to Hon. Thomas P. O'Neill, Jr., Speaker of the House of Representatives, October 1985.
4. There have been at least 150 national and state commission studies on public education reform since 1983, but the major commission reports that initially set the parameters of the debate and have most influenced public consciousness of the issues have been:

    *A Nation at Risk: The Imperative for Educational Reform*, report of the National Commission on Excellence in Education

(Bell Commission) (Washington, D.C.: U.S. Department of Education, 1983).

*Academic Preparation for College: What Students Need to Know and Be Able to Do*, report of the College Board (New York: College Entrance Examination Board, 1983).

*Action for Excellence: A Comprehensive Plan to Improve Our Nation's Schools*, report of the Task Force on Education for Economic Growth (Denver: Education Commission of the States, 1983).

*America's Competitive Challenge: The Need for a National Response*, report of the Task Force of the Business–Higher Education Forum (Washington, D.C.: Business–Higher Education Forum, 1983).

*Educating Americans for the 21st Century*, report of the National Science Board Commission on Precollege Education in Mathematics (Washington, D.C.: National Science Board, 1983).

*Making the Grade*, report of the Twentieth Century Fund Task Force on Federal Elementary and Secondary Education Policy (New York: Twentieth Century Fund, 1983).

5. John I. Goodlad, *A Place Called School: Prospects for the Future* (New York: McGraw-Hill, 1983).

Theodore Sizer, *Horace's Compromise: The Dilemma of the American High School* (Boston: Houghton Mifflin, 1984).

6. *Barriers to Excellence: Our Children at Risk*, report of the National Board of Inquiry of the National Coalition of Advocates for Students (Boston: NCAS, 1985).

7. *Investing in Our Children: Business and the Public Schools*, statement by the Research and Policy Committee of the Committee for Economic Development (New York: CED, 1985).

8. Diane Ravitch and Chester E. Finn, Jr., "High Expectations and Disciplined Effort," in Chester E. Finn, Jr., Diane Ravitch, and Robert T. Fancher, eds., *Against Mediocrity* (New York: Holmes & Meier, 1984).

See also Diane Ravitch, "The Continuing Crisis," *American Scholar*, Spring 1984.

9. *Making the Grade*, p. 6.

10. Harold Howe II, "Education Moves to Center Stage: An Overview of Recent Studies," *Phi Delta Kappan*, November 1983, p. 172.

11. Lawrence C. Stedman and Marshall S. Smith, "Recent Reform Proposals for American Education," *Contemporary Education Review*, Fall 1983.

12. Torsten Husen, "Are Standards in U.S. Schools Really Lagging Behind Those in Other Countries?," *Phi Delta Kappan*, March 1983.

    See also Marilyn Clayton Felt, *Improving Our Schools: Thirty-three Studies That Inform Local Action* (Newton, Mass.: Education Development Center, 1985), pp. 4–6.

13. Ernest Boyer, *High School: A Report on Secondary Education in America* (Princeton, N.J.: Carnegie Foundation for the Advancement of Teaching, 1983).

    Goodlad, *A Place Called School.*

    Sizer, *Horace's Compromise.*

14. Fred Hechinger, "Schools Realize Quality Is a Requisite for Survival," *New York Times*, 15 May 1984, p. C6.

15. Statistics on drop-outs and illiteracy can be found in *Barriers to Excellence*, chap. 1.

    "High School Drop-outs: Descriptive Information from High School and Beyond," *National Center for Educational Statistics Bulletin*, November 1983 (Washington, D.C.: U.S. Department of Education).

    Jonathan Kozol, *Illiterate America* (New York: Doubleday, 1985), chap. 1.

16. *Summary Report on Racial and Ethnic High School Drop-out Rates in New York City* (New York: ASPIRA, 1983).

    *Our Children at Risk*, report of the NCAS New York Hearing on the Crisis in Public Education (New York: Advocates for Children, January 1985), pp. 42–43.

17. "Preliminary Survey of High School Completion Rates, 1979–83" (unpublished; Chicago: Designs for Change, 1984).

    See also *The Bottom Line: Chicago's Failing Schools and*

*How to Save Them* (Chicago: Designs for Change, January 1985).

## Chapter 3: Three Myths of School Performance

1. Colin Greer, *The Great School Legend* (New York: Penguin, 1972), pp. 108–109.
2. Ibid., pp. 83–86, 93.
   See also Nathan Glazer and Daniel P. Moynihan, *Beyond the Melting Pot* (Cambridge, Mass.: MIT Press, 1964).
3. *A Children's Defense Budget*, report of the Children's Defense Fund (Washington, D.C.: CDF, 1984), p. 27 and chap. 8.
4. *Thirty Years After* Brown: *Three Cities That Are Making Desegregation Work*, report of the National Education Association (Washington, D.C.: NEA, May 1984).
5. Gary Orfield, *Working Paper: Desegregation of Black and Hispanic Students for 1968–80* (Washington, D.C.: Joint Center for Policy Studies, 1982).
6. Jennifer Hochschild, *Thirty Years After* Brown (Washington, D.C.: Joint Center for Policy Studies, 1985), p. 3.
7. Larry Farmer, program director of Mississippi Action for Community Education, presentation to the Educational Visions Seminar, New World Foundation, 31 May 1984.
8. Hochschild, *Thirty Years After* Brown, pp. 3, 5.
9. Regina Kyle, ed., *Kaleidescope: Emerging Patterns of Response and Action in ECIA Case Studies of Chapter 2 in Selected States*, report of the National Institute of Education by E. H. White & Co. (Washington, D.C.: U.S. Department of Education, July 1983), cited in *Education Week*, 5 December 1984, p. 1.
10. Thomas N. Bethell, "Economic Distress: Worse Than the Numbers Suggest," *Rural Coalition Report*, no. 10, December 1984, pp. 22–23.
11. *A Policy Blueprint for Community Service and Youth Employment*, report of the Roosevelt Centennial Youth Project (New York: Eleanor Roosevelt Institute, September 1984), pp. 3, 9.

"The Youth Employment Situation," press release of the Roosevelt Centennial Youth Project, March 1984.

12. AFL-CIO Committee on the Evaluation of Work, cited in "Economy Gains but Changes," *New York Times*, 4 September 1983, p. A1.

13. "The Non-Union Edge," *New York Times*, 20 January 1985, p. D1.

14. Chart cited from Mike Davis, "The Political Economy of Late Imperial America," *New Left Review*, January 1984. His sources include data from U.S. Bureau of Labor Statistics figures cited in the following:

Valerie Personick, "The Outlook for Industry Output and Employment through 1990," *Monthly Labor Review*, August 1981.

A. F. Ehrbach, "The New Unemployment," *Fortune*, April 1981.

See also Carol Boyd Leon, "Occupational Winners and Losers," *Monthly Labor Review*, June 1982.

Robert Kuttner, "The Declining Middle," *Atlantic Monthly*, July 1983.

Gene I. Maeroff, "The Real Job Boom Is Likely to Be Low Tech," *New York Times*, 4 September 1983, p. E16.

Lester C. Thurow, "The Hidden Sting of the Trade Deficit," *New York Times*, 19 January 1986, p. F3.

15. Henry M. Levin and Russell W. Rumberger, *The Educational Implications of High Technology*, Project Report No. 83-A4, Institute for Research on Educational Finance and Governance (Palo Alto, Calif.: Stanford University, February 1983), pp. 9, 10–11.

16. Janet L. Norwood, "The Job Outlook for College Graduates through 1990," *Occupational Outlook Quarterly*, Winter 1979, pp. 2–7.

See also Maeroff, "The Real Job Boom."

17. "Democratizing competition" is a concept developed in David K. Cohen and Barbara Neufeld, "The Failure of High Schools and the Progress of Education," *Daedalus*, Summer 1981.

18. *The Unfinished Agenda*, report of the National Commission on

Secondary Vocational Education (Washington, D.C.: NCSVE, December 1984).

19. Jonathan Kozol, *Illiterate America* (New York: Doubleday, 1985), p. 5.

20. "Bishops' Pastoral: Catholic Teaching and the U.S. Economy," *Origins*, 15 November 1984, pp. 358–359.

21. Andrew Hacker, ed., *U/S: A Statistical Portrait of the American People* (New York: Penguin, 1983), pp. 134, 90.

22. *Children's Defense Budget*, p. 21.

See also *American Children in Poverty*, report of the Children's Defense Fund (Washington, D.C.: CDF, 1984).

23. Harold Hodgekinson, *All One System* (Washington, D.C.: Institute for Educational Leadership, 1985).

## Chapter 4: School Practice

1. Marilyn Clayton Felt, *Improving Our Schools: Thirty-three Studies That Inform Local Action* (Newton, Mass.: Education Development Center, 1985), p. 11.

2. Anne Bridgeman, "States Launching a Barrage of Reform Initiatives, Survey Finds," *Education Week*, 6 February 1985, pp. 1, 31.

Edward B. Fiske, "States Gain Wider Influence on School Policy," *New York Times*, 2 December 1984, p. A1.

3. *City High Schools: A Recognition of Progress*, report of the Ford Foundation (New York: Ford Foundation, 1984), p. 18.

4. Ibid., p. 68.

5. Eileen M. Foley and Susan B. McConnaughy, *Towards School Improvement: Lessons from Alternative High Schools* (New York: Public Education Association, 1982).

6. Stewart C. Purkey and Marshall S. Smith, "School Reform: The District Policy Implications of the Effective Schools Literature," *Elementary School Journal*, January 1985, p. 362.

7. John I. Goodlad, *A Place Called School: Prospects for the Future* (New York: McGraw-Hill, 1983).

Theodore Sizer, *Horace's Compromise: The Dilemma of the*

*American High School* (Boston: Houghton Mifflin, 1984).

Jere Brophy, "Classroom Management and Learning," *American Education*, March 1982.

Jere Brophy, "Classroom Organization and Management," *Elementary School Journal*, March 1983.

Barak Rosenshine, "Teaching Functions in Instructional Programs," paper presented to the National Invitational Conference of the National Institute of Education, Arlington, Va., 1982.

Thomas L. Good and D. A. Grouws, "The Missouri Mathematics Effectiveness Project," *Journal of Educational Psychology*, June 1979.

Carolyn Denham and Ann Lieberman, eds., *Time to Learn* (Washington, D.C.: National Institute of Education, May 1980).
8. Ralph Frick, "In Support of Academic Redshirting," *Education Week*, 16 January 1985, p. 24.
9. Eva Baker, "Achievement Tests in Urban Schools: New Numbers," paper presented to the National Conference on Urban Education, CEMREL, St. Louis, July 1978.

Paul Houts, *The Myth of Measurability* (New York: Hart, 1977).

Thomas Kellaghan, George Madaus, and Peter Airasian, *The Effects of Standardized Testing* (Boston: Kluwer-Nijhoff, 1982).

Deborah Meier, "Why Reading Tests Don't Test Reading," *Dissent*, Winter 1981–82.

"New Approaches to Assessing Learning," *Social Policy*, September/October 1977.
10. Purkey and Smith, "School Reform."
11. Deborah Meier, "Testing Practices: Do They Help or Hurt Our Children?," testimony before the New York Hearing of the NCAS National Board of Inquiry, cited in *Our Children at Risk*, report of the NCAS New York Hearing on the Crisis in Public Education (New York: Advocates for Children, January 1985), pp. 30, 36.
12. Emily C. Feistritzer, *The Condition of Teaching: A State by*

*State Analysis* (Princeton, N.J.: Carnegie Foundation for the Advancement of Teaching, 1983).

13. *Incentives for Excellence in America's Schools*, report of the Task Force on Merit Pay and Career Ladders of the Association for Supervision and Curriculum Development (Alexandria, Va.: ASCD, January 1985).

   See also Susan J. Rosenholtz, "Political Myths About Education Reform: Lessons from the Research on Teaching," *Phi Delta Kappan*, January 1985.

14. Gene I. Maeroff, "Improving Our Teachers," *New York Times Winter Survey of Education*, 6 January 1985, p. 35.

15. Linda Darling-Hammond, *Beyond the Commission Reports: The Coming Crisis in Teaching* (Santa Monica, Calif.: Rand Corporation, April 1984).

   Linda Darling-Hammond and Arthur E. Wise, "Teaching Standards or Standardized Teaching?," *Educational Leadership*, October 1983.

16. Rosenholtz, "Political Myths," pp. 350–351.

17. Thomas Toch, "Teacher Shortage Realities Seen Thwarting Reform," *Education Week*, 5 December 1984, p. 1.

18. *Has Title I Improved Education for Disadvantaged Students?: Evidence from Three National Assessments of Reading*, report no. S4-D5-50 of the National Assessment of Educational Progress (Denver: Education Commission of the States, April 1981).

   Robert M. Stonehill and Judith I. Anderson, *An Evaluation of ESEA Title I—Program Operation and Educational Effects: A Report to Congress* (Washington, D.C.: U.S. Department of Education, 1982).

19. *A Children's Defense Budget*, report of the Children's Defense Fund (Washington, D.C.: CDF, 1984), p. 27.

20. *Making the Grade*, report of the Twentieth Century Fund Task Force on Federal Elementary and Secondary Education Policy (New York: Twentieth Century Fund, 1983), p. 12.

21. *The Condition of Bilingual Education in the Nation, 1984* (Washington, D.C.: U.S. Department of Education, 1984).

22. *Barriers to Excellence: Our Children at Risk*, report of the Na-

tional Board of Inquiry of the National Coalition of Advocates for Students (Boston: NCAS, 1985), p. 16.

23. *Evaluation of the Impact of ESEA Title VII Spanish-English Bilingual Education Programs*, report of the American Institute of Research (Palo Alto, Calif.: AIR, 1977).

Carmen Perez et al., *Report on the Educational Programs for Students of Limited English Proficiency in New York State* (Albany, N.Y.: Bureau of Bilingual Education, N.Y.S. Department of Education, October 1980).

Isaura Santiago Santiago, *A Community Struggle for Equal Educational Opportunity: ASPIRA v. Board of Education*, OME Monograph No. 2 (Princeton, N.J.: Office of Minority Education, Educational Testing Service, 1978).

*Bilingual Education, A Fundamental Right*, report of the Washington Information Resource Center (Washington, D.C.: National Congress for Puerto Rican Rights, 1983).

Laraine Testa Zappert and B. Roberto Cruz, *Bilingual Education: An Appraisal of Empirical Research*, report of the Bay Area Bilingual Education League (Berkeley, Calif.: Bahia, 1977).

24. *1980 Elementary and Secondary School Survey* (Washington, D.C.: Office of Civil Rights, U.S. Department of Education, 1982).

See also Norm Fruchter, *Action Agenda: The Prevention of Special Education Referrals* (New York: Advocates for Children, 1983).

Nicholas Hobbs, *The Futures of Children: Categories, Labels and Their Consequences* (San Francisco: Jossey-Bass, 1975).

Donald R. Moore, *Caught in the Web* (Chicago: Designs for Change, 1983).

J. E. Yesseldyke et al., "Generalizations from Five Years of Research on Assessment and Decision-Making," *Exceptional Education Quarterly*, Spring 1983.

25. Gene V. Glass, *The Effectiveness of Four Educational Interventions*, Project Report No. 84-A19, Institute for Research on Educational Finance and Governance (Palo Alto, Calif.: Stanford University, August 1984).

See also Jeannie Oakes, *Keeping Track: How Our Schools Structure Inequality* (New Haven, Conn.: Yale University Press, 1985).

Carl A. Grant and Christine E. Sleeter, "The Educational Reports of the 1980s: A Critique of Their Treatment of Equity," in Philip G. Altbach, Gail P. Kelly, and Lois Weis, eds., *Excellence in Education: Perspectives on Policy and Practice* (New York: Prometheus, 1985).

26. N. L. Gage cited in Maeroff, "Improving Our Teachers," p. 35.


## Chapter 5: School Constituents

1. *Make Something Happen*, report of the National Commission on Secondary Education for Hispanics (Washington, D.C.: Hispanic Policy Development Project, 1984).

See also Anne Henderson, ed., *Parent Participation–Student Achievement: The Evidence Grows* (Columbia, Md.: National Committee for Citizens in Education, 1981).

Henry J. Becker and Joyce L. Epstein, *Influences on Teachers' Use of Parent Involvement at Home*, report no. 324, Center for the Social Organization of Schools (Baltimore: Johns Hopkins University, April 1982).

2. James P. Comer, *School Power* (New York: Free Press, 1980).

Wilbur Brookover et al., *School Social Systems and Student Achievement: Schools Can Make a Difference* (New York: Praeger, 1979).

3. Norm Fruchter, "The Role of Parent Participation," *Social Policy*, Fall 1984.

4. Lena Williams, "Schools Encourage Active Parent Involvement," *New York Times*, 16 January 1985, p. C10.

5. "The Chapter 1 Voucher: Just the Beginning," *Heritage Foundation Education Update*, Fall 1985.

6. The Equity and Choice Act of 1985 (TEACH), Section 560(f). The concept that publicly funded vouchers constitute individual grants and not government assistance to an educational in-

stitution has gained a legal precedent in the January 1986 Supreme Court decision *Witter v. State of Washington,* which upheld the right of a disabled person to use a state educational grant to attend a Bible school.

7. Testimony cited in *Our Children at Risk,* report of the NCAS New York Hearing on the Crisis in Public Education (New York: Advocates for Children, January 1985), pp. 27–29.

8. Pamela Varley, "Evolution of the Medford Magnet Program," *Equity and Choice,* Fall 1984.

9. Chester E. Finn, Jr., and Denis T. Boyle, "As States Take Charge of Schools: A New Plan," *New York Times Winter Survey of Education,* 6 January 1985, p. 69.

10. *Education for Democracy: Leadership for Change in the 1980s,* report of the Massachusetts Teachers Association (Boston: MTA, January 1983).

11. *American Children in Poverty,* report of the Children's Defense Fund (Washington, D.C.: CDF, 1984), p. 19.

12. The North Dakota Study Group initiated the recent report, *Education for a Democratic Future,* statement of the Public Education Information Network (St. Louis: Campus Box 1183, Washington University, 1985).

13. Matthew B. Miles, Eleanor Farrar, and Barbara Neufeld, *The Extent of Adoption of Effective Schools Programs,* report prepared for the National Commission on Excellence in Education (Cambridge, Mass.: Huron Institute, January 1983).

14. Larry Cuban, "Transforming the Frog into a Prince: Effective Schools Research, Policy, and Practice at the District School Level," *Harvard Education Review,* May 1984.

15. Stewart C. Purkey and Marshall S. Smith, "School Reform: The District Policy Implications of the Effective Schools Literature," *Elementary School Journal,* January 1985.

16. Ibid., pp. 358–359.

17. Anna Lou Pickett, "The Paraprofessional Movement: An Update," *Social Policy,* Winter 1983–84.

18. *The Human Factor: A Key to Excellence in Education,* report of

the National Association of Social Workers (Silver Spring, Md.: NASW, February 1985).

Comer, *School Power*, chap. 7.

19. *A Review of Head Start Research since 1970* (Washington, D.C.: Office of Human Development Services, U.S. Department of Health and Human Services, September 1983).

20. Kamer Davis, *Adult Literacy: Study of Community Based Literacy Programs* (Washington, D.C.: Association for Community Based Education, September 1983).

21. Thomas Bethell, "Crippling the American Conservation Corps," *Rural Coalition Report*, no. 10, December 1984.

22. *A Policy Blueprint for Community Service and Youth Employment*, report of the Roosevelt Centennial Youth Project (New York: Eleanor Roosevelt Institute, September 1984).

## Chapter 6: Governance and Funding

1. Rick Atkinson, "Segregation Rises Again in Many Southern Schools," *Washington Post*, 1 April 1984, p. A1.

2. Jennifer Hochschild, *Thirty Years After* Brown (Washington, D.C.: Joint Center for Policy Studies, 1985).

3. P. Berman cited in Stewart C. Purkey and Marshall S. Smith, "School Reform: The District Policy Implications of the Effective Schools Literature," *Elementary School Journal*, January 1985.

4. John Augenblick, "The States and School Finance: Looking Back and Looking Ahead," *Phi Delta Kappan*, November 1984.

   See also Edward B. Fiske, "States Gain Wider Influence on School Policy," *New York Times*, 2 December 1984.

5. Anne Bridgeman, "States Launching a Barrage of Reform Initiatives, Survey Finds," *Education Week*, 6 February 1985, pp. 1, 31.

6. "Changing Course: A Fifty State Survey of Reform Measures," *Education Week*, 6 February 1985, pp. 11–30.

   Anne Bridgeman et al., "Governors Outline Education Agenda," *Education Week*, 16 January 1985, pp. 8, 14.

7. Louis Grumer, New York State School Boards Association, cited in Fiske, "States Gain."
8. Bridgeman, "States Launching."
   See also *The Nation Responds: Recent Efforts to Improve Education* (Washington, D.C.: U.S. Department of Education, May 1984).
9. Hochschild, *Thirty Years After* Brown, p. 41.

## Chapter 7: Building a New Agenda

1. Thomas N. Bethell, "Now Let's Talk About Jobs Again," *Rural Coalition Report*, no. 10, December 1984, p. 11.

# Bibliography

This bibliography lists both the principal sources cited in this book and selected works that provide background for the topics we have covered. We have arranged the listing by chapter, to indicate where each work has particular value in the school reform debate, although readers will find many works useful in several areas of the discussion.

## Chapter 2: The Mission of Schooling

The major commission reports that were instrumental in sparking the excellence movement include:

*Academic Preparation for College: What Students Need to Know and Be Able to Do*, report of the College Board. New York: College Entrance Examination Board, 1983.

*Action for Excellence: A Comprehensive Plan to Improve Our Nation's Schools*, report of the Task Force on Education for Economic Growth. Denver: Education Commission of the States, 1983.

*America's Competitive Challenge: The Need for a National Re-*

*sponse,* report of the Task Force of the Business–Higher Education Forum. Washington, D.C.: Business–Higher Education Forum, 1983.

*Educating Americans for the 21st Century,* report of the National Science Board Commission on Precollege Education in Mathematics. Washington, D.C.: National Science Board, 1983.

*Making the Grade,* report of the Twentieth Century Fund Task Force on Federal Elementary and Secondary Education Policy. New York: Twentieth Century Fund, 1983.

*A Nation at Risk: The Imperative for Educational Reform,* report of the National Commission on Excellence in Education (Bell Commission). Washington, D.C.: U.S. Depa:tment of Education, 1983.

Useful summaries of recent reports and studies include:

Felt, Marilyn Clayton. *Improving Our Schools: Thirty-three Studies That Inform Local Action.* Newton, Mass.: Education Development Center, 1985.

McNett, Ian. *Charting a Course: A Guide to the Excellence Movement in Education.* Washington, D.C.: Council for Basic Education, 1984.

*A Summary of Major Reports on Education.* Denver: Education Commission of the States, November 1983.

Critical reviews of the national reports include:

Cross, Patricia. "The Rising Tide of School Reform Reports," *Phi Delta Kappan,* November 1984.

Giroux, Henry. "Public Philosophy and the Crisis in Education," *Harvard Education Review,* May 1984.

Grant, Carl A., and Christine E. Sleeter. "The Educational Reports of the 1980s: A Critique of Their Treatment of Equity," in Philip G. Altbach, Gail P. Kelly, and Lois Weis, eds., *Excellence in Education: Perspectives on Policy and Practice.* Buffalo, N.Y.: Prometheus, 1985.

Hacker, Andrew. "The Schools Flunk Out," *New York Times Book Review,* 12 April 1984.

Howe, Harold, II. "Education Moves to Center Stage: An Overview of Recent Studies," *Phi Delta Kappan*, November 1983.

Husen, Torsten. "Are Standards in U.S. Schools Really Lagging Behind Those in Other Countries?," *Phi Delta Kappan*, March 1983.

Peterson, Paul. "Did the Education Commissions Say Anything?" *Brookings Review*, Winter 1983.

Pincus, Fred L. "From Equity to Excellence: The Rebirth of Educational Conservatism," *Social Policy*, Winter 1984.

Stedman, Lawrence C., and Marshall S. Smith. "Recent Reform Proposals for American Education," *Contemporary Education Review*, Fall 1983.

Toch, Thomas. "The Darker Side of the Excellence Movement," *Phi Delta Kappan*, November 1984.

Studies and commentary that have been central in developing both sides of the debate include:

Boyer, Ernest. *High School: A Report on Secondary Education in America*. Princeton, N.J.: Carnegie Foundation for the Advancement of Teaching, 1983.

*The Education Crisis: Washington Shares the Blame*. Washington, D.C.: Heritage Foundation, May 1984.

Finn, Chester E., Jr., Diane Ravitch, and Robert T. Fancher, eds. *Against Mediocrity*. New York: Holmes & Meier, 1984.

Goodlad, John I. *A Place Called School: Prospects for the Future*. New York: McGraw-Hill, 1983.

*Investing in Our Children: Business and the Public Schools*, a statement by the Research and Policy Committee of the Committee for Economic Development. New York: Committee for Economic Development, 1985.

Ravitch, Diane. "The Continuing Crisis," *American Scholar*, Spring 1984.

Sizer, Theodore. *Horace's Compromise: The Dilemma of the American High School*. Boston: Houghton Mifflin, 1984.

*Toward More Local Control: Financial Reform for Public Education*, final report of the Advisory Panel on Financing Elementary and Secondary Education (Marshner Commission). Washington, D.C.: U.S. Department of Education, December 1982.

Other sources on the crisis of inequity in schooling include:

*American Children in Poverty.* Washington, D.C.: Children's Defense Fund, 1984.

*Barriers to Excellence: Our Children at Risk,* report of the National Board of Inquiry of the National Coalition of Advocates for Students. Boston: National Coalition of Advocates for Students, 1985.

*The Bottom Line: Chicago's Failing Schools and How to Save Them.* Chicago: Designs for Change, January 1985.

*A Children's Defense Budget.* Washington, D.C.: Children's Defense Fund, 1984.

Cole, Beverly P. "The State of Education for Black Americans," in *Education 84/85: Annual Editions.* Guilford, Conn.: Dushkin, 1984.

"High School Drop-outs: Descriptive Information from High Schools and Beyond," *National Center for Educational Statistics Bulletin*, November 1983. Washington, D.C.: U.S. Department of Education.

Hochschild, Jennifer. *Thirty Years After* Brown. Washington, D.C.: Joint Center for Policy Studies, 1985.

Kyle, Regina, ed. *Kaleidoscope: Emerging Patterns of Response and Action in ECIA Case Studies of Chapter 2 in Selected States,* report of the National Institute of Education by E. H. White & Co. Washington, D.C.: U.S. Department of Education, July 1983.

*Make Something Happen,* report of the National Commission on Secondary Schooling for Hispanics. Washington, D.C.: Hispanic Policy Development Center, December 1984.

Oakes, Jeannie. *Keeping Track: How Schools Structure Inequality.* New Haven, Conn.: Yale University Press, 1985.

*Our Children at Risk,* report of the NCAS New York Hearing on the Crisis in Public Education. New York: Advocates for Children, January 1985.

*Saving the African American Child,* report of the Task Force on Black Academic and Cultural Excellence. Washington, D.C.: National Alliance of Black School Educators, November 1984.

*Summary Report on Racial and Ethnic High School Drop-out Rates in New York City.* New York: ASPIRA, 1983.

## Chapter 3: Three Myths of School Performance

Sources on school history and development include:

Bowles, Samuel, and Herbert Gintis. *Schooling in Capitalist America.* New York: Basic Books, 1976.

Cohen, David K., and Barbara Neufeld. "The Failure of High Schools and the Progress of Education," *Daedalus,* Summer 1981.

Cremin, Lawrence. *The Transformation of the School.* New York: Vintage, 1964.

deLone, Richard H. *Small Futures: Children, Inequality, and the Limits of Liberal Reform.* New York: Harcourt Brace Jovanovich, 1979.

Greer, Colin. *The Great School Legend.* New York: Penguin, 1972.

Ogbu, John. *Minority Education and Caste.* New York: Academic Press, 1978.

Popkewitz, Thomas B., Robert Tabachnick, and Gary Wehlage. *The Myth of Educational Reform.* Madison, Wisc.: University of Wisconsin Press, 1980.

Ravitch, Diane. *The Troubled Crusade: American Education, 1945–80.* New York: Basic Books, 1983.

Sarasen, Seymour B. *The Culture of the School and the Problem of Change.* Boston: Allyn & Bacon, 1971.

Tyack, David B. *The One Best System.* Cambridge, Mass.: Harvard University Press, 1974.

Sources on the current economic and social contexts of schooling include:

*An Analysis of the Impact of Reagan Economic Policies on Female-Headed Households.* Washington, D.C.: Center on Budget and Policy Priorities, October 1984.

## Bibliography

Blumberg, Paul. *Inequality in an Age of Decline.* New York: Oxford University Press, 1980.

Hodgekinson, Harold. *All One System.* Washington, D.C.: Institute for Educational Leadership, 1985.

Kuttner, Robert. "The Declining Middle," *Atlantic Monthly,* July 1983.

Leon, Carol Boyd. "Occupational Winners and Losers," *Monthly Labor Review,* June 1982.

Levin, Henry M., and Russell W. Rumberger. *The Educational Implications of High Technology,* Project Report 83-A4, Institute for Research on Educational Finance and Governance. Palo Alto, Calif.: Stanford University, February 1983.

Maeroff, Gene I. "The Real Job Boom Is Likely to Be Low Tech," *New York Times,* 4 September 1983.

Norwood, Janet L. "The Job Outlook for College Graduates through 1990," *Occupational Outlook Quarterly,* Winter 1979.

Personick, Valerie. "The Outlook for Industry Output and Employment through 1990," *Monthly Labor Review,* August 1981.

*The Unfinished Agenda,* report of the National Commission on Secondary Vocational Education. Washington, D.C.: NCSVE, December 1984.

## Chapter 4: School Practice

Sources listed for Chapter 2 cover many of the instructional reform issues discussed in this chapter. Additional sources listed here are also applicable in many instances to the discussion of teacher empowerment in Chapter 5.

Brophy, Jere. "Classroom Management and Learning," *American Education,* March 1982.

Brophy, Jere. "Classroom Organization and Management," *Elementary School Journal,* March 1983.

*City High Schools: A Recognition of Progress.* New York: Ford Foundation, 1984.

Darling-Hammond, Linda. *Beyond the Commission Reports: The*

*Coming Crisis in Teaching.* Santa Monica, Calif.: Rand Corporation, April 1984.

Darling-Hammond, Linda, and Arthur E. Wise. "Teaching Standards or Standardized Teaching?," *Educational Leadership,* October 1983.

Denham, Carolyn, and Ann Lieberman, eds. *Time to Learn.* Washington, D.C.: National Institute of Education, May 1980.

*Education for a Democratic Future,* statement of the Public Education Information Network. St. Louis: Washington University, 1985.

Feistritzer, Emily C. *The Condition of Teaching: A State by State Analysis.* Princeton, N.J.: Carnegie Foundation for the Advancement of Teaching, 1983.

Foley, Eileen M., and Susan B. McConnaughy. *Towards School Improvement: Lessons from Alternative High Schools.* New York: Public Education Association, 1982.

Frick, Ralph. "In Support of Academic Redshirting," *Education Week,* 16 January 1985.

Glass, Gene V. *The Effectiveness of Four Educational Interventions,* Project Report No. 84-A19, Institute for Research on Educational Finance and Governance. Palo Alto, Calif.: Stanford University, August 1984.

Good, Thomas L. "How Teacher Expectations Affect Results," *American Education,* December 1982.

Good, Thomas L., and D. A. Grouws. "The Missouri Mathematics Effectiveness Project," *Journal of Educational Psychology,* June 1979.

*Incentives for Excellence in America's Schools,* report of the Task Force on Merit Pay and Career Ladders of the Association for Supervision and Curriculum Development. Alexandria, Va.: ASCD, January 1985.

Maeroff, Gene I. "Improving Our Teachers," *New York Times Winter Survey of Education,* 6 January 1985.

Raywid, Mary Anne, Charles A. Tesconi, Jr., and Donald R. Warren. *Pride and Promise: Schools of Excellence for All the People.*

Westbury, N.Y.: American Educational Studies Association, November 1984.

Rosenholtz, Susan J. "Political Myths About Education Reform: Lessons from the Research on Teaching," *Phi Delta Kappan*, January 1985.

Rosenshine, Barak. "Teaching Functions in Instructional Programs," paper presented to the National Invitational Conference of the National Institute of Education, Arlington, Va., 1982.

"Schools That Work," *New York Times Spring Survey of Education*, 15 April 1984.

Sources on the impact of standardized testing include:

Baker, Eva. "Achievement Tests in Urban Schools: New Numbers," paper presented to the National Conference on Urban Education, CEMREL, St. Louis, July 1978.

Houts, Paul. *The Myth of Measurability*. New York: Hart, 1977.

Kellaghan, Thomas, George Madaus, and Peter Airasian. *The Effects of Standardized Testing*. Boston: Kluwer-Nijhoff, 1982.

Meier, Deborah. "Why Reading Tests Don't Test Reading," *Dissent*, Winter 1982–83.

"New Approaches to Assessing Learning," *Social Policy*, September/October 1977.

Weber, George. *Uses and Abuses of Standardized Testing in the Schools*, Occasional Paper No. 22. Washington, D.C.: Council for Basic Education, 1978.

Studies on the impact of compensatory education include:

*Has Title I Improved Education for Disadvantaged Students?: Evidence from Three National Assessments of Reading*, report no. S4-D5-50 of the National Assessment of Educational Progress. Denver: Educational Commission of the States, April 1981.

Stonehill, Robert M., and Judith I. Anderson. *An Evaluation of ESEA Title I—Program Operation and Educational Effects: A Report to Congress*. Washington, D.C.: U.S. Department of Education, 1982.

Studies on the impact of bilingual education include:

*Bilingual Education: A Fundamental Right*, report of the Washington Information Resource Center. Washington, D.C.: National Congress for Puerto Rican Rights, 1983.

*The Condition of Bilingual Education in the Nation, 1984*. Washington, D.C.: U.S. Department of Education, 1984.

*Evaluation of the Impact of ESEA Title VII Spanish-English Bilingual Education Programs*, report of the American Institute of Research. Palo Alto, Calif.: AIR, 1977.

Perez, Carmen, et al. *Report on Educational Programs for Students of Limited English Proficiency in New York State*. Albany, N.Y.: Bureau of Bilingual Education, N.Y.S. Department of Education, October 1980.

Santiago, Isaura Santiago. *A Community Struggle for Equal Educational Opportunity: ASPIRA v. Board of Education*, OME Monograph No. 2. Princeton, N.J.: Office of Minority Education, Educational Testing Service, 1978.

Zappert, Laraine Testa, and B. Roberto Cruz. *Bilingual Education: An Appraisal of Empirical Research*, report of the Bay Area Bilingual Education League. Berkeley, Calif.: Bahia, 1977.

Studies on the impact of special education for students with handicapping conditions include:

Fruchter, Norm. *Action Agenda: The Prevention of Special Education Referrals*. New York: Advocates for Children, November 1983.

Hobbs, Nicholas. *The Futures of Children: Categories, Labels, and Their Consequences*. San Francisco: Jossey-Bass, 1975.

Moore, Donald R. *Caught in the Web*. Chicago: Designs for Change, 1983.

*1980 Elementary and Secondary School Survey*. Washington, D.C.: Office of Civil Rights, U.S. Department of Education, 1982.

Yesseldyke, J. E., et al. "Generalizations from Five Years of Research on Assessment and Decision-Making," *Exceptional Education Quarterly*, Spring 1983.

**Bibliography**

## Chapter 5: School Constituents

Sources that address parent and citizen involvement include:

Becker, Henry J., and Joyce L. Epstein. *Influence on Teachers' Use of Parent Involvement at Home*, Report No. 324, Center for the Social Organization of Schools. Baltimore: Johns Hopkins University, April 1982.

Brookover, Wilbur, et al. *School Social Systems and Student Achievement: Schools Can Make a Difference.* New York: Praeger, 1979.

Comer, James P. *School Power.* New York: Free Press, 1980.

Fruchter, Norm. "The Role of Parent Participation," *Social Policy,* Fall 1984.

Henderson, Anne, ed. *Parent Participation–Student Achievement: The Evidence Grows.* Columbia, Md.: National Committee for Citizens in Education, 1981.

Commentary on voucher systems includes:

Bridgeman, Anne, and Cindy Currence. "Voucher Ideas Floated," *Education Week,* 16 January 1985.

"The Chapter 1 Voucher: Just the Beginning," *Heritage Foundation Education Update,* Fall 1985.

Cohen, David K. "Reforming School Politics," *Harvard Education Review,* November 1978.

Coons, John E., and Stephen D. Sugarman. *Education by Choice: The Case for Family Control.* Berkeley, Calif.: University of California Press, 1978.

Finn, Chester E., Jr., and Denis T. Boyle. "As States Take Charge of Schools: A New Plan," *New York Times Winter Survey of Education,* 6 January 1985.

Varley, Pamela. "Evolution of the Medford Magnet Program," *Equity and Choice,* Fall 1984.

Sources on the Effective Schools movement include:

*California School Effectiveness Study (1974–75).* Sacramento, Calif.: State of California Department of Education, 1977.

Cuban, Larry. "Transforming the Frog into a Prince: Effective Schools Research, Policy, and Practice at the District Level," *Harvard Education Review*, May 1984.

Edmunds, Ronald. "Effective Schools for the Urban Poor," *Educational Leadership*, October 1979.

Fruchter, Norm. *A Discussion of Local School Improvement.* New York: Metropolitan Educational Development and Research Project, Fall 1982.

Miles, Matthew B., Eleanor Farrar, and Barbara Neufeld. *The Extent of Adoption of Effective Schools Programs*, report prepared for the National Commission for Excellence in Education. Cambridge, Mass.: Huron Institute, January 1983.

Purkey, Stewart C., and Marshall S. Smith. "School Reform: The District Policy Implications of the Effective Schools Literature," *Elementary School Journal*, January 1985.

Rutter, Michael, et al. *Fifteen Thousand Hours.* Cambridge, Mass.: Harvard University Press, 1979.

"Special Issue on School Effectiveness," *Social Policy*, Fall 1984.

Weber, George. *Inner City Children Can Be Taught to Read.* Washington, D.C.: Council for Basic Education, 1971.

Zerchykov, Ross, ed. *Citizens' Notebook for Effective Schools.* Boston: Institute for Responsive Education, 1984.

Sources on community-school linkages and youth service include:

*Education for Democracy: Leadership for Change in the 1980s*, report of the Massachusetts Teachers Association. Boston: MTA, January 1983.

Gittell, Marilyn, and Janice Moore. *Educational Opportunity and Community Service: The Community Based College.* New York: Ford Foundation, November 1983.

*Giving Youth a Better Chance: Options for Education, Work, and Service.* San Francisco: Carnegie Council on Policy Studies in Higher Education, 1979.

*The Human Factor: A Key to Excellence in Education*, report of the National Association of Social Workers. Silver Spring, Md.: NASW, February 1985.

Pickett, Anna Lou. "The Paraprofessional Movement: An Update," *Social Policy*, Winter 1983–84.

*A Policy Blueprint for Community Service and Youth Employment*, report of the Roosevelt Centennial Youth Project. New York: Eleanor Roosevelt Institute, September 1984.

*A Review of Head Start Research since 1970*. Washington, D.C.: Office of Human Development Services, U.S. Department of Health and Human Services, September 1983.

Commentary on literacy and community-based literacy programs includes:

Davis, Kamer. *Adult Literacy: Study of Community Based Literacy Programs*. Washington, D.C.: Association for Community Based Education, September 1983.

Hunter, Carmen, and David Hartman. *Adult Illiteracy in America*. New York: McGraw-Hill, 1979.

Kozol, Jonathan. *Illiterate America*. New York: Doubleday, 1985.

Spangenburg, Gail. *Adult Illiteracy in America*. New York: Carnegie Corporation of New York, September 1981.

## Chapter 6: Governance and Funding

Sources cited in Chapters 2 and 5 also reflect on governance issues; the commission studies cited throughout have particular funding implications. Other sources not yet mentioned include:

Atkinson, Rick. "Segregation Rises Again in Many Southern Schools," *Washington Post*, 1 April 1984.

Augenblick, John. "The States and School Finance: Looking Back and Looking Ahead," *Phi Delta Kappan*, November 1984.

Bridgeman, Anne. "States Launching a Barrage of Reform Initiatives, Survey Finds," *Education Week*, 6 February 1985.

Bridgeman, Anne, et al. "Governors Outline Education Agenda," *Education Week*, 16 January 1985.

"Changing Course: A Fifty State Survey of Reform Measures," *Education Week*, 6 February 1985.

Fantini, Mario, Marilyn Gittell, and Richard Magat. *Community Control in the Urban School.* New York: Praeger, 1970.

Fiske, Edward B. "States Gain Wider Influence on School Policy," *New York Times,* 2 December 1984.

Fuhrman, Susan, and Alan Rosenthal, eds. *Shaping Education Policy in the States.* Washington, D.C.: Institute for Educational Leadership, 1981.

Garms, Walter I., and James W. Guthrie. *School Finance.* Englewood Cliffs, N.J.: Prentice-Hall, 1978.

Gittell, Marilyn, "The 'New' Federalism and Old Politics: Their Impact on Urban Education," in Alan Gartner, Colin Greer, and Frank Riessman, eds., *What Reagan Is Doing to Us.* New York: Harper & Row, 1982.

Gittell, Marilyn. "School Governance," in Charles Brecher and Raymond D. Horton, eds., *Setting Municipal Priorities.* Totowa, N.J.: Allanheld, Osmun, 1981.

Kirst, Michael W. "The Changing Balance in State and Local Power to Control Education," *Phi Delta Kappan,* November 1984.

*The Nation Responds: Recent Efforts to Improve Education.* Washington, D.C.: U.S. Department of Education, May 1984.

Odden, A., and V. Dougherty. *State Programs for School Improvement: A Fifty State Survey.* Denver: Education Commission of the States, 1982.

*Thirty Years After* Brown: *Three Cities That Are Making Desegregation Work.* Washington, D.C.: National Education Association, May 1984.

Zerchykov, Ross, ed. *School Boards and the Communities They Represent: An Inventory of the Research.* Boston: Institute for Responsive Education, 1984.

# About the Authors

ANN BASTIAN is a program associate at the New World Foundation and also a college teacher and labor analyst.

NORM FRUCHTER is an education consultant and a school board member of Community School District 15 in Brooklyn.

MARILYN GITTELL is a professor of political science at the Graduate Center, City University of New York.

COLIN GREER is president of the New World Foundation and an education historian.

KENNETH HASKINS is co-director of the Principals Center of the Graduate School of Education, Harvard University.

# Index

# Index